D1561127

To George "Big Foot,"

Hope you enjoy
the memories —
Go Cleveland!
Best Wishes.
George Cormack

On the Front Cover: Looking Toward Public Square, 1930 (See P. II)

Published by:

INSTANT CONCEPTS, INC.
CLEVELAND OFFICE
440 Beeler Drive
Berea, OH 44017

•

Columbus
4856 Sawmill Road PMB 341
Columbus, OH 43235

•

(440) 891-1964 • FAX (440) 826-1920

NATIONWIDE: 1-800-644-7769

e-mail: calendar@infinet.com

•

Copyright © 1999 by Instant Concepts, Inc.

Printed in the United States of America. All rights reserved.
No part of this book may be reproduced or utilized in any form or by any means, electronic or mechanical,
including photocopying, without prior written permission of the author, except in the case of brief quotations
embodied in critical articles and reviews. All facts have been researched by the author and to the best of the
author's knowledge are accurate.

First Printing • April, 1999
Second Printing • October 1999

Electronic Pre-Press:
Camelot Typesetting, Cleveland, Ohio

ISBN 1882171-19-5

About the Editor

George Cormack is a 1971 graduate of Berea High School in Berea, Ohio and a 1977 graduate of Ohio State University. Mr. Cormack is also a member of the Western Reserve Historical Society, the Society of American Baseball Research (SABR) and the Berea Historical Society.

About Memories of a Lifetime- Vol. 1

The Cleveland Press Collection at Cleveland State University is the source for all photographs found in this edition. Every attempt has been made to ensure the accuracy of the information found in this publication. Passages from newspaper accounts have been marked by quotation marks. For space considerations,"The Cleveland Press," has been shortened to "The Press," in most accounts. Unfortunately, we regret that errors and omissions do occur. Should you have any questions about the material or information contained within, or have information or photographs that can be used in further editions, please do not hesitate to call Instant Concepts.

About Instant Concepts, Inc.

Instant Concepts, Inc. is a historical research and marketing company specializing in the publication of historical books and calendars. Instant Concepts has published collector edition History of Cleveland and Cleveland Sports History calendars since 1993. Some back issues of these publications are still available through the publisher. Instant Concepts released its first book edited by Mr. Cormack, "Municipal Stadium, Memories on the Lakefront, Vol. 1," in November of 1997.

Instant Concepts actively collects historical information, photographs on regional, national and international events and personalities, and maintains an ever-growing electronic database of over 12,000 historical entries.

About the Front Cover

The RKO Hippodrome Theater featured "Mammy," starring Al Jolson, a movie billed by the theater as "A Joyous Jolson Jubilee, Jokes, Jazz and Jollity- a feast of frolicsome fun and Irving Berlin's greatest hits," on Thursday, June 19, 1930, when the unique view of Euclid Avenue looking toward Public Square was published in The Cleveland Press. The scene was captured from a traffic tower about to be dismantled by city workers that stood in the middle of the busy thoroughfare at E. Ninth Street.

In The Press on June 19th, Rosen Motors, 6201 Euclid Avenue, offered a used 1929 Durant 66 sedan with 4-speed transmission for $695, on terms of 5% down and no mortgage on furniture; while Towell Cadillac, Chester and E. 30th, advertised a 1929 La Salle Town Sedan for $1,859, a 1926 Chevrolet Coupe for $97, a 1923 Peerless Victoria for $129 and a 1929 Packard limousine for $1,491. A. L. Englander Motor Co. offered a 1929 Ford Model A coupe for $575.

The following day, four trains of 100 double-length railway cars brought the world famous Ringling Bros., Barnum & Bailey Circus to town for a two-day stay. The company's 42 elephants helped 800 "stake men" pitch the 31-tent "canvas city" of the Greatest Show On Earth along the lakefront just west of E. Ninth Street. Featured among the "human attractions" were a tribe of "genuine monster-mouthed" Ubangi savages from the French Congo, Hugo Zachinni, "who is shot from the mouth of a stage gun," the Wallendas, "dome-high thrillers of the steel thread," and Luicita Leers, "Europe's greatest aerialist."

By the end of the month, the complexion of downtown Cleveland would be forever changed. On June 24, 1930, ground was broken for the city's new Municipal Stadium along the lakefront. On June 28, 1930, the Van Sweringen's massive Union Terminal project on Public Square was formally dedicated.

Memories of A Lifetime

VOLUME 1

Featuring over 600 images from The Cleveland Press Collection

This book is dedicated to the thousands of wonderful folks who have shared their personal recollections of Cleveland with me throughout the years, and to the many personalities, from all walks of life, who have added so much to the fascinating history of Cleveland. I can only hope that the wonderful array of photographs and stories found within trigger memories that can be shared with friends, family members and students in classrooms throughout America. I also hope that my work triggers more historical discovery.

This book is also dedicated to the many people who have given me the chance to make such an important addition to Cleveland's proud history possible and to the photographers who fought the elements, and at times their editors, to bring us these images. Understanding the determination and resolve represented by the people featured within, where giving up was never an option, moved me to tears several times while putting this project together. Looking back at history should always be a humbling experience.

Rather than limit this edition to a particular period of time, this book has been designed to be much like the old Cleveland Press newspaper, with separate sections on entertainment, politics, sports, etc., allowing the greatest array of photographs possible without constraint.

I personally thank William Becker, University Archivist, Cleveland State University, who has been an immense help in putting this project together; Tom Poole, Bryan Rapp, Rick Colby, Joe Mengel and Marilyn & Paul Wieber for their support. A final thanks goes out to the city's radio stations, who played some really great tunes, especially good old rock-n-roll, while I was putting this book together. Life doesn't get much better than listening to Billy Bass deliver the oldies while writing about the days of WIXY-1260 "Super Radio." I still have old 45's in a "Disc-o-Case" from the early 60's, won as the 12th caller to WIXY's hot line during one of the station's weekend "battle of the bands!"

Best Wishes,

George Cormack
Editor
Memories of a Lifetime- Vol. 1

A special dedication goes out to the thousands of American men and women who have served, or are serving, in our nation's military, too many times losing their lives while fighting to protect our freedom. As we prepare to enter the new millennium, I hope their efforts have been worth the cost.

Sections In This Edition

October 2, 1930

PUBLIC SQUARE UPON PRESIDENT HOOVER'S ARRIVAL

After arriving with his wife by train on Thursday, October 2, 1930, President Herbert Hoover headed to Public Square for a 1 P.M. private luncheon with 250 bankers at Hotel Cleveland. That afternoon, The Press reported, "Public Square held a crowd that had swarmed all over Soldiers and Sailors Monument, had clambered to first floor ledges of surrounding business blocks and was bulging far back into the tributary thorofares." Hoover was also scheduled to speak before the American Banker's Association convention that evening at Public Hall. While the president dined with the nation's bankers, Mrs. Hoover was the guest of honor at a Women's City Club luncheon hosted by 250 area women. The United States Navy band performed on Public Square that afternoon and at Public Hall before Hoover's evening presentation. That night, Hoover told the nation's bankers, "American standards of living must be maintained. We shall need mainly to depend on our own strong arm."

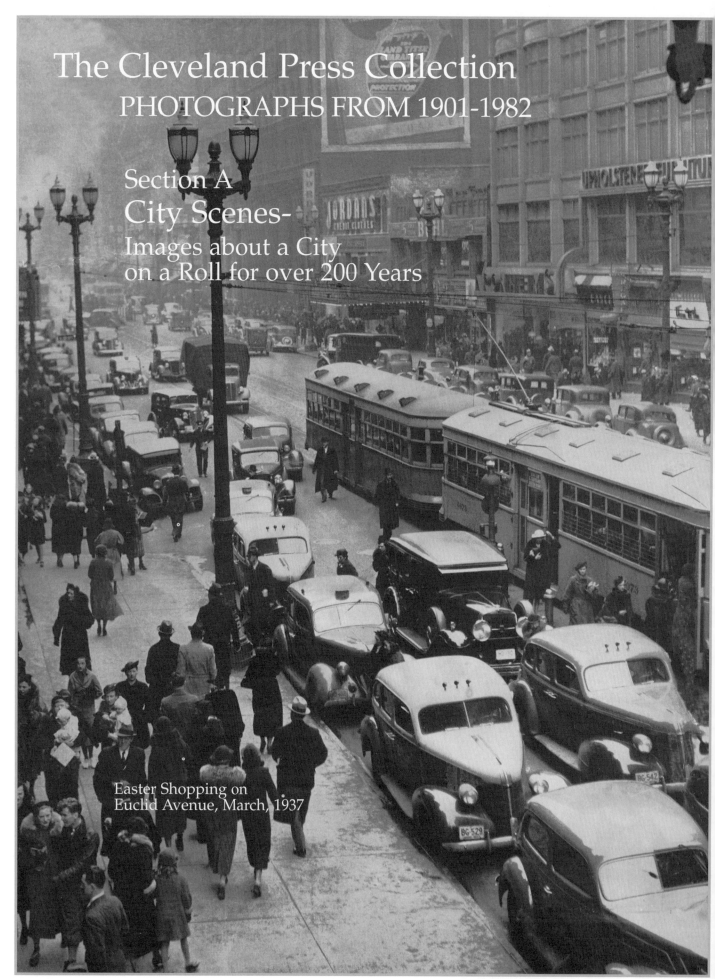

The Cleveland Press Collection
PHOTOGRAPHS FROM 1901-1982

Section A
City Scenes-
Images about a City
on a Roll for over 200 Years

Easter Shopping on
Euclid Avenue, March, 1937

(Right) E. 4TH & EUCLID AVE., February 1, 1928

After the city released a report evaluating the hubs of downtown street car traffic, The Press reported on Wednesday, February 1, 1928 that the findings were favorable to existing rapid transit plans, stating, "Ten years ago more people boarded and left street cars at E. 13th Street and Euclid avenue, than any other point in the entire city. Today, this greatest inpouring and outpouring of carriders is (at right), at E. Fourth Street and Euclid avenue." The high-traffic intersection was only blocks from where a street car hub was planned for the Van Sweringen's new Union Terminal project on Public Square.

(Below right) PLAYHOUSE SQUARE, August 3, 1940

The weekend fare for theater goers along Euclid Avenue at busy Playhouse Square on Saturday, August 3, 1940 included "All This and Heaven Too," starring Bette Davis and Charles Boyer at the Allen Theater; "When The Daltons Rode," featuring Randolph Scott at the R-K-O Palace and "Untamed," with Ray Milland and Patricia Morrison at Loew's State. Starting at the Allen on Saturday, August 10th was "The Great Walt Disney Festival of Hits," featuring five animated films, "Show White and the Seven Dwarfs;" "Ferdinand The Bull;" The Three Little Pigs in "Practical Pig;" "The Ugly Duckling" and "Donald's Lucky Day."

(Above) THE MILK FUND CAMPAIGN, April 5, 1932

"The girls deposited their coins and then slid to happiness," reported The Press on Tuesday, April 5, 1932, as the young women below posed on a slide attached to the giant milk bottle in Public Square. The bottle was being used to raise money for the city's school milk fund campaign.

Cleveland, Ohio
May, 1922

August, 1922

OPPOSITE PAGE- CLEVELAND 1922 (Left) Public Hall, upon its opening on April 22, 1922 as the newest addition to the city's growing downtown landscape. **(Left below)** Public Square from the Illuminating Building in August of 1922. Shortly afterward, demolition began on the square's southwest corner eventually giving way to the Van Sweringen's ambitious new Terminal Tower project.

(Right) A STREETCAR TIE-UP, May 9, 1945

When a streetcar derailed on Euclid Ave. in front of the May Co. on Wednesday, May 9, 1945, catching a ride became a bit more difficult the day after VE-Day.

(Below) PUBLIC SQUARE, September 1, 1949

As the city prepared to host the 40th anniversary edition of the National Air Races over the busy Labor Day weekend on Thursday, September 1, 1949, streetcars, autos and busses joined pedestrian traffic in providing a sometimes confusing array of congestion around hectic Public Square. At the time, city leaders were debating raising parking tickets from $1 to $2.

May, 1945

September, 1949

(Below) PLAYING JACKS ON PROSPECT AVE., July 16, 1948

"Cleveland's newest residential area is downtown," wrote Press staffer Alex Groner on Friday, July 16, 1948, describing how evicted families were moving into second and third rate downtown hotels and housekeeping rooms in the shadow of Terminal Tower. "Children, quick to adjust to a faster tempo, learn to dodge traffic, dart in and out of doorways and alleys and grow wary of street perils," Groner reported. **(Below)** Lillyan Hagashi, 11 (center), and Patricia Kroyer, 12 (right), convert the sidewalk on Prospect Avenue into a playground. The girls resided with their families at nearby Hotel Talgarth.

(Above) AT THE TOM JOHNSON STATUE, July 2, 1931

The out of work men above at the Tom Johnson statue on Public Square sweltered in the summer heat with temperatures above the 90° mark on Thursday, July 2, 1931. The next night, the city hosted its first major event, a boxing match, at new Municipal Stadium.

(Left)
ALL-NATIONS FESTIVAL, August 17, 1949

More than 5,000 children enjoyed a day of fun and games during the city's annual playground day program on Wednesday, August 17, 1949. After forming at E. 13th Street and Chester Avenue, the youngsters marched to Euclid Ave. and down Euclid through Public Square to the Mall, where a series of playground contests and demonstrations were staged including a kite flying contest and a "most freckles" contest. **(Left)** The Mall crowd is entertained by gaily-costumed folk dancers participating in the afternoon togetherness. The Press Showagon and Traveling Zoo were also important elements of the youth parade and festive Mall program.

THE PARADE OF PROGRESS
Sunday, April 27, 1952

More than 250,000 lined the street six-deep from E. 21st to the Mall during the city's Parade of Progress on Sunday April 27, 1952, held to mark the conversion of Euclid Avenue from streetcars to busses. The next day, Press columnist Bill Barrett wrote, "Euclid Avenue was a weary but happy old lady today, basking in the warmest memories of her proud history. The biggest crowd that ever swarmed downtown on a Sunday afternoon lined the curbs yesterday to pay homage to her past and salute her future." Barrett added, "A light breeze ruffled the colorful costumes of the marchers and the spring finery of the folks watching," including the thousands at left, who brought the street alive "with spring color from curb to curb." The nostalgic tribute included antique cars, League of Women Voters volunteers dressed as "suffragettes," and even a horse-drawn streetcar. The next day, another fleet of busses began providing service to riders along Euclid Avenue, bringing the number of downtown lines on the main artery to 11.

AMERICAN LEGION PARADE, September 27, 1920

The American Legion began their second annual national convention, the first held in Cleveland, on Monday, September 27, 1920, with the 20,000-member parade at left which traveled along Euclid Avenue from E. 40th to Public Square. The Press reported that day, "At the head of the parade marches a group of men whose personal bravery in the face of greatest danger, has been recognized by awards of the Congressional Medal of Honor."

Here Comes the Parade!

THE NRA PARADE, August 1, 1933

Over 30,000 spectators converged on Public Square to witness the noon-time National Recovery Act (NRA) parade held to celebrate the beginning of the city's NRA drive on Tuesday, August 1, 1933. **(Right)** After starting their trek at E. 21st and Euclid Avenue, marchers pass by a huge honor roll billboard as painters add the names of some 4,000 employers who had already signed NRA agreements with the Emergency Campaign Commission of Re-employment.

West Side Market

"The gilded dome gleamed hopefully above the unfinished West Side marketplace Thursday," offered The Press in the story that ran with the photograph at left on Thursday, September 19, 1912. The article about when the $684,000 project would open continued, "For nearly two years, the dome has been radiating hope. For a good deal longer, 14 years in fact, Westsiders have been bathed in hope. And now comes the hopeful announcement the market will positively be opened soon." At 10 A.M. on Saturday, November 2, 1912, Market Master Kamp declared the 110-stand market open for business "as the fragrance of flowers mingled with the smell of sausages and cheese." Shoppers flocked to shop at the spotless marble counters, "where dealers wrapped up meats, groceries and other produce to the strains of "Everybody Doing It," "Dixie," and other airs played by Kirk's Military band." The next morning, The Cleveland Leader reported, "A person boarding a West Side streetcar had to run the gamut of market baskets nine out of ten people were carrying with them. Not all the marketers came on the street car, however. Automobiles rolled up to the market house and dealers declared that they were receiving a share of East Side patronage."

**(Left) THE NEW FISH MARKET,
May 9, 1915**

On Wednesday, May 9, 1915, The Press reported that city Park Supt. Alber had received a letter from world-famous food expert Dr. Harvey Wiley who requested photographs and data about the market's newly-opened fish market at left for an article in Good Housekeeping Magazine. At the time, the seven-stand market was the only one of its kind in the nation.

CELEBRATING 50 YEARS OF SERVICE, September 24, 1962

As the West Side Market prepared to begin its 50th anniversary celebration the following week, on Monday, September 24, 1962, The Press published the photographs above honoring arcade merchants (left), and original tenants inside the market (right), who were celebrating 50 years of service. While some began working at the market as youngsters, others were selling cheeses, meats, poultry, dairy products, fruits, flowers and vegetables from their stalls when the market opened in 1912.

(Right) THANKSGIVING DINNER
November 25, 1931

Biting cold winds were predicted for Thanksgiving Day as the shoppers at right gathered "fixins" for their holiday meals on Wednesday, November 25, 1931. "Turkeys gobbled, ducks quacked and geese squawked their swan songs at Central Market today," offered The Press with the photograph at right. Geese were selling for 18¢, chickens 24¢, turkeys 32¢ and little pigs 35¢. That evening, as housewives began preparing their family feasts, the four Marx brothers were appearing at the R-K-O Palace on Playhouse Square, while the Hippodrome Theater featured a special midnight preview of the thriller "Frankenstein" starring Boris Karloff. Thanksgiving Day football contests included former stars of Shaw High and Cleveland Heights High playing at Shaw Stadium to raise money for needy families, John Carroll battling the U. S. Marines at Municipal Stadium and Western Reserve taking on Ohio Wesleyan at League Park.

Central Market

A DAY AT CENTRAL MARKET
August 20, 1940

The city's ancient Central Market served an estimated 75,000 shoppers each week when The Press published the photographs above and right on Tuesday, August 20, 1940. Lacking running water or any refrigeration, the 84-year-old frame structure was embroiled in controversy, as some wanted to leave it alone, while others wanted the fire hazard torn down allowing area traffic to flow more efficiently. **(Above)** Curb stalls, though vital to the market's success, pushed into the streets restricting traffic around the marketplace. **(Above right)** An aerial shot of the market area taken from the Terminal Garage, looking south up Ontario with Broadway and Woodland leading away. **(Right)** Shoppers support one of the 322 merchants housed inside the market.

Built at a cost of $5,407,000, the Detroit-Superior High Level Bridge opened to streetcar traffic on December 24, 1917. Twelve concrete arches and one 591-foot steel arch spanned the Cuyahoga River, making the 3,112-foot span the largest double-deck, reinforced concrete bridge in the world when it opened.

UNDER CONSTRUCTION
circa 1903

(Below left) TRAFFIC CONGESTION, April 4, 1938

While getting to town was an easy process for Detroit-Superior Bridge travelers on Monday, April 4, 1938, getting home became more difficult with a lane closed to traffic.

The Detroit-Superior Bridge

(Below) TRAFFIC CONGESTION, June 17, 1952

Concerned about the high volume of traffic crossing the Detroit-Superior Bridge, Mayor Thomas A. Burke held a special meeting with Cleveland Transit System officials on Tuesday, June 17, 1952, hoping to convince CTS that some of its Detroit-Superior bus traffic (below), should be rerouted onto the nearby Lorain-Carnegie span.

The Lorain-Carnegie Bridge

COMPLETING THE PYLON, July 13, 1932

As work on the Lorain-Carnegie bridge neared completion on Wednesday, July 13, 1932, workers secured the head on one of the bridge's four massive art deco pylons. Made of Berea sandstone, each pylon was designed to symbolize a step in the progress of transportation. When the span crossing the Cuyahoga River opened later that year, drivers at first shunned the structure because of the congestion they found at both ends. In 1936, the bridge was recognized for its outstanding architecture by the American Institute of Steel Construction. On September 1, 1983, after a three-year renovation, the bridge was renamed the Hope Memorial Bridge in honor of Cleveland-native Bob Hope and his father Harry, one of the stone cutters on the original project.

CROSSING THE OLD MAIN AVENUE BRIDGE

As the traffic at right tried to cross the Main Ave. Bridge on Saturday, July 15, 1933, the workers below right were forced to turn the bridge manually after a freighter damaged the aging structure. At far right, cars cross the Main Avenue Bridge five years later on April 6, 1938, just before work on replacing the span began.

BUILDING A NEW BRIDGE (Below left) "The $6,000,000 Main Avenue Bridge is moving forward with the demolition of homes and the building of giant piers," reported The Press on Tuesday, June 21, 1938, as it described a number of WPA projects taking place throughout Greater Cleveland. **(Below)** "It was a union that stirred the throng of watchers which had been gathering all through the morning," Press reporter Robert Bordner wrote on Tuesday, May 23, 1939, after the two ends of the $7,000,000 Main Avenue Bridge were joined at 11:32 A.M., 150 feet above the Cuyahoga River. Press photographer Fred Bottomer balanced on the steel structure to capture the image.

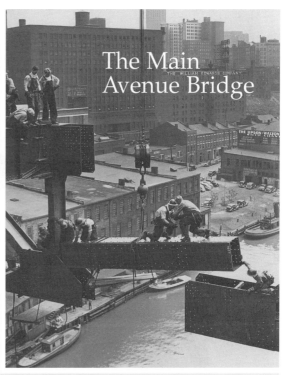

The Main Avenue Bridge

(Left) DEDICATING THE BRIDGE, October 6, 1939

Over 100,000 enthusiastic revelers brought a holiday spirit to the opening of the Main Street Bridge on Friday, October 6, 1939. **(Far left)** As part of the dedication celebration, a parade of some 10,000 marchers offered a spectacular display of military, fraternal and labor organizations under the illumination of the bridge's new sodium lights. As loud speakers carried the ceremonies to the onlookers on the bridge, WHK Radio carried the dedication activities to the nation. **(Above left)** County Commissioner John F. Curry looks on as County Commissioner John F. Gorman christens the new bridge by smashing a champagne bottle with a hammer as Miss Bernadine Koman, Cleveland Fashion Institute queen for 1938, holds the bottle.

Mrs. J. Rene and Dolly Smith
AT EDGEWATER PARK
June 23, 1927

Capitalizing on the popularity of America's newest little sweetheart, a Shirley Temple look-a-like contest was held at Music Hall on Thursday, February 7, 1935, as part of the city's annual Food Show at Public Hall. The "Press Food Show Movie Double Contest," began calmly, with 949 young hopefuls vying for the $50.00 grand prize. But soon, mothers began pushing and shoving their way to the judging area, many times getting separated from their dimpled darlings wearing "those copyrighted Shirley Temple plaid dresses."

The Shirley Temple Look-A-Like Contest

February 7, 1935

After the wildly-confusing beginning, a four-judge panel sifted through the pint-sized entries all afternoon before inviting 175 "ladies ages 3 to 6," back for the finals that evening. Lois Mae Krieger, a 6-year-old with "light curls, a nice smile and a delightful lack of affection," was the unanimous choice, much to the dismay of fifty vocal mothers who stayed for the finals. Their response prompted Press reporter Ben Williamson to write, "One dissenting mother said things that bring long suspensions to baseball players when baseball players say such things to umpires." Williamson added at the end of his story, "Lois Mae and the other top two were their spry selves as their pictures were taken. The judges pleaded fatigue and went off and had a drink I suspect. Having stood around for nearly five hours of the day with the Shirlies, I wondered how the children could still be spry. For cuteness in carload lots is a little wearing."

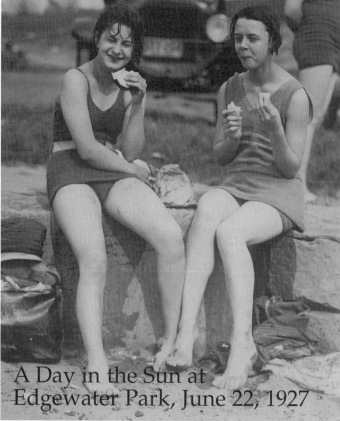

A Day in the Sun at Edgewater Park, June 22, 1927

Despite the decree by Cleveland Park Director Frank S. Harmon "that no one-piece or light-colored suits may appear on the public bathing beaches this year," as rising temperatures ushered in the start of summer on Wednesday, June 22, 1927, the bathers at left and above spent the day at Edgewater Park, frolicking on the beach and in the refreshing waters of Lake Erie. On Tuesday, June 28th, the Cleveland Orchestra, under the direction of Rudolph Ringwall, christened the park's new bandstand with the first of a five-week series of summer pops and symphonic concerts at Edgewater and Gordon parks. Wednesday was designated as "Nationality Night," when "airs of the different nations represented in Cleveland's population," were played.

When Edgewater Park's new $150,000 bathhouse at right opened in May of 1912, it was called the finest of its kind in the country. The massive steel and concrete structure featured locker rooms for 8,000, a third-floor deck, showers, a lunch room and concession stands. In 1930, bathing suits could be rented for 10¢. But by 1940, bathhouse revenues for the season dropped to $490.00, forcing the city to close the structure the following year. By 1949, the bathhouse was in such disrepair that Mayor Thomas A. Burke ordered the building torn down.

The Edgewater Park Bathhouse

More than 15,000 German-American men, women and children traveled to Edgewater Park on Sunday, June 20, 1932, for the annual German Day celebration sponsored by the Federation of German Organizations of Greater Cleveland. Mayor Ray T. Miller began the event by joining federation president Otto L. Fricks in addressing the impressive gathering. **(Above)** The Mayerbeer Orchestra under the direction of former Washington Symphony conductor Rudolph Shueller provides the musical background for a chorus of men and women selected from local German organizations under the direction of Arthur Nusser. **(Right)** The elaborate program included folk dancing by area groups garbed in brightly colored original costumes representing Bavarian, Saxon and other German people; athletic contests, and the gymnastic exhibitions at right, performed by the Germania Turn Club directed by Gustave Bachman, and the Socialer Turn Club, directed by Carl Hein. The day-long festivities ended with a dance at Siebenbuerger Saxons Hall, 7001 Denison Ave. S. W.

German Day
at Edgewater Park
June 20, 1932

"At intervals, organist Warren Steffen announces a whistle-drawback waltz and everyone changes partners. This gets the club chummy," club president Erving Hancy told Press reporter Jack Warfel for a story about the Fellowship Defense Skating Club (below right), published on Saturday, November 8, 1941. The group of "nocturnal makers of ammunition and weapons ages 18 to 50," met at Rollercade, said to be the largest unobstructed roller rink in America, on Tuesday and Thursday from 10:30 A.M. to 12:30 A.M. for informal skating sessions. Otis Steel, U. S. Aluminum, Republic Steel, Warner and Swasey, National Acme, General Electric, Thompson Products and Baltimore and Ohio Railroad were among the plants represented by fellowship skaters.

At The Rollercade
W. 68th St. & Dennison   November, 1941

(Right)
STRIKING STEEL WORKERS MEET, September 22, 1919

As a strike against the nation's steel companies began on Monday, September 22, 1919, area steel workers were organized for a mass rally at Brookside Park in support of the strike. Over 10,000 local workers (at right just before the meeting began), stood in a drizzling rain to hear speeches by local leaders including Henry W. Raisse, secretary of the organization committee, who told attendees, "The steel trust octopus has been exploiting employees long enough." Among the local plants affected were American Steel and Wire Co., Otis Steel Co., McKinney Steel Co., Bourne-Fuller Co., and Empire Rolling Mills.

Brookside Park

The First Night Game at Brookside Park

SUNDAY, May 22, 1938

"They spread out a lot, leaving room for overflowing parts of the body that would be closely confined in a stadium with seats, but there certainly were a powerful lot of people dotting the steep slopes of Cleveland's famous natural amphitheater," wrote Press Sports Editor Stuart Bell on Monday, May 23, 1938, after an estimated 80,000 spectators, the largest local sandlot crowd in 25 years, attended the first night game played at Brookside Park on Sunday, May 22nd. Eight poles equipped with 100 bulbs of 1,500 watt power, "chased every bit of darkness from the playing field." The debut of nocturnal play in Cleveland Baseball Federation's Class A division began at 8 P.M. with CBF chairman I. S. (Nig) Rose introducing Mayor Harold H. Burton, CBF president William T. Duggan, Tris Speaker, Doik Novario, Julius Kemeny, J. Noble Richards, Pete Johns, Dr. C. J. Sterling and Sam James; Parks Director Hugh Varga, Max Rosenblum and WGAR sportscaster Franklin (Whitey) Lewis. The Poschke Barbecues maintained their grasp on first place in Class A play, defeating Lyon Tailors, 5-2, as Jim Vacha outpitched Art Tomson for the win. Poschke second-baseman Ray (Mack) Mlckovsky, who went 3 for 4, became the first player to hit a night homer at Brookside Park, belting a solo blast in the bottom half of the first inning. Three hours earlier, 62,244 watched manager Oscar Vitt's first-place Cleveland Indians belt eleven hits to beat the second-place N. Y. Yankees, 8-3, at Municipal Stadium. Tribe starter Mel Harder hurled a complete game for the win, holding Joe DiMaggio, Red Rolfe, Babe Dahlgren and Bill Dickey hitless. Bell wrote in his column, "Cleveland may be one of the focal points of the recession, but it stood up nobly yesterday in offering turnstile fodder."

WHERE THE BATHHOUSE STOOD, June 14, 1918

When the photograph at right appeared in The Press on Friday, June 14, 1918, it appeared with the photograph below showing where a bathhouse appeared on the burnt timbers jutting into the Lake Erie two weeks earlier. Fire destroyed the park's massive bathhouse, leaving bathers without a place to change until new facilities were built. "If you want to go bathing at Gordon Park, you'll have to get into your suit at home," the paper reported. When the new changing area was completed, it included 552 lockers for women and 1,952 for men. The paper also reported that Parks Director Waite had no new regulations about the length, style, or shape of bathing suits for 1918 stating, "He contends Cleveland bathers are 'ladies and gentlemen' and need no specific restrictions placed on their costumes."

SUNDAY IN THE SUN, July 17, 1932

"Mr. and Mrs. Cleveland-And All the Children-Enjoyed Sunday Out of Doors," offered The Press headline on Monday, July 18, 1932, above the photograph at right showing "pleasure craft of all descriptions," travelling along the canal that connected Gordon Park lagoon with Lake Erie. The Press teamed with the City Parks Department on that summer Sunday to sponsor a free concert at the Gordon Park bandshell featuring the 75-piece accordion band of the Wurlitzer Studios for Advancement of Music. The special entertainment was arranged by the mayor's recreation committee for the city's unemployed.

Gordon Park

SUNDAY DRIVING, August 19, 1945

As the end of World War II brought the lifting of gas rationing, The Press reported on Monday, August 20, 1945, "Contrary to popular expectation, the accident toll was surprising low," after area Clevelanders, including those at right heading west-bound along the shore at Gordon Park, traveled with new found freedom. The paper added, "Motorists took advantage of bright summer skies and full gasoline tanks to hit the highways of Greater Cleveland yesterday in the first peacetime Sunday driving since the nation went to war." Police estimated that traffic on local thoroughfares was at least 50 per cent more than on the wartime Sundays of the previous four years. While ration boards processed the flood of applications for new tires, gas stations were reporting a heavy increase in tire repairs, as area drivers were forced to ride on tires "at the junking stage." One overburdened station turned away 25 cars limping in with flat tires.

CONGESTION ON THE HILL, April 25, 1929

"Cleveland Heights women's clubs and civic groups are urging construction of a street car subway under Cedar Hill to eliminate traffic congestion," reported The Press on Thursday, April 25, 1929, as area residents expressed their growing concern over the growing traffic menace at right along Cedar Road during the rush hour "crush." The traffic problem was compounded by streetcars from the Cedar-Lee line crossing Cedar at the top of the hill.

(Left) AT SHOREGATE SHOPPING CENTER, 1955

Attracting young autograph seekers to Shoregate Shopping Center in July of 1955 were Cleveland Indians outfielder Gene Woodling (left), and highly-touted rookie left-hander Herb Score (center). After a successful minor league career, Score won American League Rookie-of-the Year honors that season.

East Side

(Left) THE PRESS SHOWAGON, June 16, 1958

The crowd at left was attending the first Press Showagon performance of the summer at Woodland Hills Park on Monday, June 16th, 1958. Joe Baldi and his orchestra provided the musical background as twenty acts of amateur entertainers successfully overcame opening-night jitters to deliver their song, dance and comedy routines. For the next ten weeks, The Press Showagon and Traveling Zoo traveled each weekday to neighborhood locations throughout Cleveland. The shows were sponsored by The Press, Recreation Council and Cleveland Zoo.

THE UNIVERSITY CIRCLE AREA, February 19, 1955

The city's internationally recognized Cleveland Orchestra was preparing to begin its 25th year of performances at Severance Hall (domed building center), when the aerial view of the University Circle/Wade Park area at left, appeared in The Press on Saturday, February 19, 1955. Guiding the Cleveland Orchestra was maestro George Szell, who was marking his 10th year as musical director. At far left is the Cleveland Museum of Art which opened in 1918. February 19, 1955 was also the day an energetic young singer named Elvis Presley first appeared in Cleveland. Presley, performing for the first time north of the Mason-Dixon line, was brought in by local promoter Syd Friedman as part of the traveling Louisiana Hayride troupe for a one-night, two-show performance at the Circle Theater, E. 101st and Euclid Avenue. Presley returned to Cleveland a second time that year, appearing in October at Brooklyn High School.

THE SHAKER SQUARE FESTIVAL, June 26, 1933

Performances by the championship Cleveland Heights High School Band highlighted entertainment enjoyed by attendees taking part in the Shaker Square Festival on Monday, June 26, 1933. The day-long community affair included a 1 P.M. children's style show sponsored by Higbee's at Shaker Tavern, followed by a dance program sponsored by the Billy Tilton School of Dancing. At 3 P.M., the Heights High band conducted the first of three concerts. The action continued at 6:30 P.M., with a Twilight League baseball game between Cleveland Bronze and Ohio Bell Telephone Company, followed that evening by street dancing, more band concerts and free movie showings.

Shaker Square

CELEBRATING 30 YEARS, September 10, 1959

On Thursday, September 10, 1959, The Press published a special feature highlighting Shaker Square's 30th anniversary, opened in the spring of 1929 by the Van Sweringen brothers, Orris and Mantis, as the Midwest's first integrated shopping center. The colonial building occupied by popular Stouffer's restaurant at right, once housed the Shaker Tavern.

Pat O'Brien at the New Colony Theater

The film, "It's Love I'm After," starring Bette Davis, Leslie Howard and Olivia De Haviland served as the opening night attraction when Warner Brothers opened its new Colony Square Theater at Shaker Square, complete with RCA high fidelity sound and air-flow seats, on Tuesday, December 28, 1937. Mrs. Douglas Brien, winner of a contest to name the movie house, cut the ribbon to open the chain's 452nd theater.

(Right) To promote the opening, Warner Bros. movie star Pat O'Brien (fifth from left), visited the theater on Monday, Dcember 20, 1937. O'Brien was in town to emcee the annual Cleveland Press Christmas Charity Show at Public Hall.

PLAN NOW TO ATTEND THE GALA PREMIERE OPENING Of *Warner Bros.* COLONY THEATRE TUESDAY DEC. 28th FREE PARKING ON PREMISES

December 20, 1937

**(Left)
GLINKA'S TAVERN,
NEWBURGH HTS.,
1953**

The teens at left danced to hits from the juke box outside Ray Glinka's Tavern, 3972 E. 42nd St., Newburgh Heights, in May of 1953. At the time, The Press was celebrating the 65th anniversary of the juke box with one of their Hit Tune Parties at Public Hall on Saturday, May 10th. Featured at the Hit Tune concert were Decca recording star Connee Boswell; Hamish Menzies, whose first waxing "Less than Tomorrow" was a nationwide hit; local polka star Johnnie Pecon and the bands of Ray Anthony and Sammy Watkins. The Hit Tune for May on area juke boxes was Buddy Greco's Coral recording of "You're Driving Me Crazy."

West Side

Lakewood Community Days- The Parades of Children

JULY 29, 1941

While Cleveland Heights residents were participating in the city's ninth annual community carnival at Cain Park on Tuesday, July 29, 1941, the city of Lakewood held its annual Parade of Children on Lake Avenue as a prelude to its 9th annual Community Festival the next day. Winning prizes for their parade participation were Kathryn and Joan Seltzer, Doll Buggies; Natalie and Donna Habert, Pets; Patty and Peggy Holly, Costumes; Jack Reitz, Richard Fisher, Jack Gundrum and Shirley Smith, Floats; Beverly Baker and Myrtle Mayshort, Bicycles; and John Reilly, Soap Boxes.

JULY 28, 1943

Lakewood police estimated that 15,000 turned out for the city's 11th annual Community Day on Wednesday, July 28, 1943, which climaxed with the annual parade of children at left along Clifton Avenue. During the parade, a group of youngsters dressed as nurses raised $100 for the Red Cross from money thrown into the large white bed sheet they carried.

At Parmadale...

(Right) CELEBRATING THE FEAST OF CORPUS CHRISTI, June 19, 1927

Thousands of Cleveland Catholics traveled to Parmadale on Sunday, June 19, 1927, for the annual celebration of the Feast of Corpus Christi, held under the auspices of the Catholic District League and the Women's District League. Bishop Joseph Schrembs of the Roman Catholic Diocese of Cleveland pronounced the benediction of the Blessed Sacrament at the four altars in the village and also preached a sermon. Trustees of the Catholic Charities Corporation served as the bearers of the canopy in the procession at right. Music was furnished by the Parmadale boys' choir, St. Francis male quartet and Parmadale boys' band.

(Right) HOSTING THE MARBLES TOURNEY, May 7, 1928

Parmadale youngsters carry some of the eats served to contestants on Monday, May 7, 1928, during the competition to pick Parmadale's representative at the Sixth Annual Press Marbles Tournament.

(Far right) KIDS' WEEK, December 16, 1929

The youngsters at far right were among 350 Parmadale youth attending the first day of Kids' Show Week sponsored by The Press and the Cleveland Federation of Women's Clubs at the R-K-O Palace on Monday, December 16, 1929. Over 2,500 disadvantaged youth were expected to attend the special holiday matinees.

(Right) WITH FATHER FLANAGAN, May 4, 1939

"But jimminy crickets, it did happen today- yes siree!- the biggest day of all the big days! Father Flanagan of Boys Town came to Parmadale," wrote Press reporter Robert H. Clifford after the famed priest came to Parmadale on Thursday, May 4, 1939, to help open the annual fund raising campaign of the Catholic Charities Corp. Upon his arrival, he was greeted by some 400 young men including the group at right with "Rags" the dog. After surveying the 160-acre site, Father Flanagan remarked, "It is an ideal setup for a children's village. It is far superior to mine." That night, the head of Boys Town spoke before the most enthusiastic pre-campaign rally ever assembled to open the charity drive. Nearly 1,600 attended the banquet, including Auxiliary Bishop James A. McFadden.

Section C
Business

Pride-
A Word
Used with
Dignity by
the Workers
of Cleveland

AT JONES AND LAUGHLIN, June, 1958
The Cleveland Press reported on Thursday, June 19, 1958, "The seven
o'clock whistle is blowing again at Jones and Laughlin's Cleveland
plant. It's a happy sound to those who have been called back to work.

(Right) GRASSELLI CHEMICAL CO. WORKS, Circa 1901

With the death of his father in 1882, Caesar Augustine Grasselli took over operation of the Grasselli Chemical Co. and the chemical works (at right), located in the flats near E. 26th St. and Independence Rd. By 1885, the company was a leading chemical manufacturer with Standard Oil of Ohio among its major accounts. In 1885, Grasselli introduced the production of domestic saltcake (sodium sulfate) for the glass injury. He also introduced the manufacture of acetic acid in 1902, developed and improved the process for producing ammonia in 1903, and introduced the production of silicate of soda for the manufacture of soap. During World War I, the Grasselli Chemical Co. was instrumental in the production of explosives for the war effort. On November 10, 1928, the company's board of directors approved a merger with E. I. DuPont de Nemours Co. of Wilmington, Delaware.

(Right) CORRIGAN, MCKINNEY STEEL CO., November 12, 1926

"A new chapter is written in Cleveland's history of steel," wrote Press reporter Harold G. McCoy on Friday, November 12, 1926, after the new 10-inch rolling plant of the Corrigan, McKinney Steel Co., a year in building, was placed in operation. For the first time in local history, steel could be forged in one plant from "ore of Michigan mines," to the finished bar. At right, some of the 75 workers employed at the plant fill 3 1/2 ton ingot molds. The new plant, completely operated by electricity, was fitted to deliver a daily supply of 400 tons of steel bars in different shapes.

(Right) AT THE FISHER BODY PLANT, January 11, 1939

At Englander Pontiac, 7200 Euclid Avenue, new Pontiacs began at $758.00, when the photograph of the Fisher Body workers at right was published in The Press on Wednesday, January 11, 1939. The huge Cleveland plant of the Fisher Body Division of General Motors Corp., which began operations in 1921, covered 40 acres on E. 140th Street. With over 1.4 million feet of floor space, the massive facility, with some three miles of conveyor belts, was capable of producing 5,000 bodies daily from over 12,000 tons of steel used on a monthly basis.

AT THE FORD MOTOR FOUNDRY, December 28, 1964

Press reporter Julian Krawcheck began his Monday, December 28, 1964 story on the city's automobile industry with, "A lot of automobiles have passed over the pike since 1904, when a Cleveland-made Peerless was delivered to John D. Rockefeller at his home in Forest HIlls. The oil king paid $5,000 for the stately limousine, nurturing a baby Cleveland industry which has grown to astonishing size in 60 years." At the time of Krawcheck's story, Greater Cleveland ranked as the nation's second-largest automotive center, with 95,000 workers or roughly 25% of the area's work force employed by the auto industry. **(Left)** Moulding line workers in December of 1964, pouring metal for engine parts at Ford's Cleveland Casting Plant in Brook Park, Ohio.

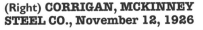

The White Motor Co.

(Right)
AT THE WHITE MOTORS PLANT, May 10, 1928

Reporter Paul Packard wrote in The Press on Thursday, May 10, 1928, "(Thomas H.) White had been working in a chair factory for $1.25 a day. But during his spare moments he experimented with a sewing machine. In 1859, he was granted patents on his invention, a small hand-propelled machine with a single thread stitch. Thus began the organization which today employs more than 6,000 workers with a manufacturing plant in Cleveland consisting of 26 buildings with a total floor space of 1,531,781 square feet." At right, Mike Wosar (left), William Molohan and William Frolich work on the White
Motors assembly line in 1928, "where trucks were built to last from 100,000 to 500,000 miles." The first company to purchase a White truck was the Denver Dry Goods Co., which bought a White steam truck in 1900.

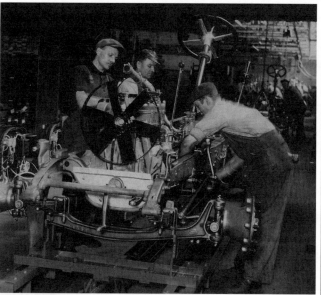

White Workers Welcome Dorothy Lamour

May 2, 1942

"Like a good soldier, she made all the trips which her Cleveland Federation of Labor hosts had planned for her despite the fact that she was nearly exhausted from lack of sleep," reported The Press on Saturday, May 2, 1942, after Hollywood starlet Dorothy Lamour spent the day in Cleveland selling war bonds. Lamour visited a number of local plants including Warner and Swasey, Westinghouse Electric Co., and White Motors, where Army "half tracs" were produced. Above right, the actress posed with machine operator Earl Wrobbel as she toured the White Motors facility with White president Robert F. Black. Lamour also attended a 1 P.M. bond rally that day at Public Square.

(Left) APPLYING AT THE CADILLAC TANK PLANT, August 21, 1950

Applicants began lining up at 3:45 A.M. on Monday, August 21, 1950, for one of 6,000 positions offered by Cadillac Tank Plant officials at the former bomber plant. By noon, officials had handed out over 8,000 applications.

(Above) M-41 tanks built at the massive West Side facility near the airport.

"We chose Cleveland as the site of our most modern store because this is the place we began and because we have always been well received here," vice president J. W. Connors remarked as Bond's prepared to open its new $1 million clothes store (below), at E. Ninth and Euclid on Wednesday, October 15, 1947. A Press poll found that three out of four respondents liked the new structure. While one person polled said of the Walker and Weeks-designed building, "It makes Cleveland seem less like a village and more like New York," a negative respondent stated, "It looks like a graham cracker."

(Below) Store manager A. L. Petrie (left), appears before the store opening with some of the store's newly-hired staff on the store's 'floating staircase.'

Opening the New Bond Store
October, 15, 1947

DONATING BLOOD FOR OUR FIGHTING MEN, March 16, 1943

"The recruiting job took only a couple of days, since people were anxious to do their share," reported advertising director Lloyd Rosenblum, after the Rosenblum's employees and store management below organized a mass blood donation on Tuesday, March 16, 1943. "A number of our employees conceived the idea of making a group donation and asked the help of Max Rosenblum, our treasurer," Rosenblum added. After donating blood for America's fighting men at the Red Cross Blood Donor Center, 3111 Prospect Ave., some for the fourth or fifth time, Rosenblum's continued the "Donor Party" by providing dinner for the generous blood givers.

(Right) UNION TRUST OPENS, May 19, 1924

When the Union Trust Company opened its new 20-story, 1.178-million-square-foot headquarters at the corner of E. Ninth St. and Euclid Avenue on Monday, May 19, 1924, the downtown Cleveland intersection was said to be the third busiest intersection in the nation. At right, first day visitors were photographed in the Union Trust Building's main lobby, called "the greatest banking room in the world."

Banking in Cleveland

(Left) CENTRAL UNITED NATIONAL BANK, March 13, 1933

Central United National Bank at 308 Euclid Avenue on Monday, March 13, 1933, the day "the largest national bank in Ohio," joined Cleveland Trust, National City Bank and Society of Savings as one of four local financial institutions reopened by federal regulators in 12 key cities during the Bank Holiday of 1933.

(Right) GETTING THE LATEST FINANCIAL NEWS, June 25, 1962

Mrs. Darrell Biemot of Bache & Co. marks the hourly movement of the Dow Jones Industrial stock average on Tuesday, June 25, 1962 in the window of National City Bank at E. Sixth and Euclid Avenue. Developed in cooperation with local investment companies, the latest financial news was displayed daily along with items pertinent to business and financial trends. The young ladies outside the window were representatives of Prescott & Company and Goodbody & Company.

The Union and Guardian Trust Banks Reopen, July 25, 1933

On Tuesday, July 25, 1933, hundreds of residents crowded outside Union Trust bank at E. Ninth and Euclid, and Guardian Trust Co. bank on Prospect Avenue, for their share of the more than $53,000,000 in payoff checks about to be issued to customers with deposits at the city's second and third largest banks. Union Trust depositors received 35 per cent of their deposits, while Guardian customers received a 20 percent payoff. As depositors secured their money, downtown retailers reported heavy customer counts as many came in to pay outstanding bills. Several stores had arranged for special booths to cash payoff checks. "People are buying heavily," said William Gray, secretary of the Retail Credit Association. "Many people who got their payoff checks today evidently are using the money to pay off old bills, many three or four months standing," Gray added. At the same time, Corliss E. Sullivan, chairman of the board of the Central United National Bank reported, "Our percentage of new business is very good." Local banks enjoyed a substantial increase in new deposit activity because of the bank payoff.

(Above right) Anxious depositors waited outside Union Trust at E. Ninth and Euclid for the bank to open its doors. The payoff began at 8:50 A.M., when the bank opened 10 minutes early to prevent the crowd from spilling into the intersection.

(Right) By mid-morning, some 2,000 depositors crowded into the massive Union Trust lobby, standing in alphabetically-arranged lines for their payoff checks.

(Below) Depositors outside Guardian Trust waiting for the bank to open. Nearly 26,000 bank patrons were expected to receive their dividends by the end of the day.

(Below right, Far right) Depositors in the Guardian Trust lobby on July 25th.

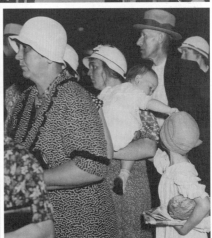

The Richman Brothers Co.

AT THE RICHMAN BROTHERS PLANT, March 17, 1927

THE NEW RICHMAN BROTHERS CO. STORE, May 14, 1927

The Richman Brothers Co. opened its second downtown store on Saturday, May 14, 1927, in the former Vincent-Barstow Building at 725-731 Euclid Avenue. The six-story, 70,000 square foot outlet (below), featured a 10,000-piece selection of wool suits, topcoats and three-piece tuxedos with silk dress vests, all at one affordable price-$22.50. The new store was reported to be the largest of its kind devoted strictly to men's fashions.

AT THE RICHMAN BROTHERS FACTORY, 1600 E. 55TH, March 17, 1927

As the clothier prepared to open it new flagship store on Euclid near E. Ninth St., a special feature in The Press on Friday, March 17, 1927, began with, "Time clocks and foremen have no place in the organization of Richman Bros. Co., manufacturers of men's clothes." Included in the special section were the photographs below and right. **(Below)** The tailors in the finishing shop below were among over 1,500 workers employed at the Richman Brothers manufacturing plant on E. 55th St. in 1927. **(Right)** Workers at play behind the Richman Brothers plant.

(Right) CELEBRATING RICHMAN BROTHERS' 55TH ANNIVERSARY, November 28, 1934

A Thanksgiving feast with all the trimmings awaited Richman Brothers employees as they celebrated the company's 55th anniversary on Wednesday, November 28, 1934 at the Richman factory on E. 55th St.

(Left) RICHMAN EMPLOYEES RECEIVE THEIR BONUS CHECKS, December 19, 1941

The U. S. Civil Service Commission was looking for a minimum of 523 local lads to help rebuild recently-bombed Pearl Harbor on Friday, December 19, 1941, when a front page headline in The Press offered, "War, Sure, But No Blackout on Holiday Spirit." At left, Santa Claus (James Makin), presents bonus checks to Richman Brothers employees on the 19th during the clothing manufacturer's annual Social Club party on the fifth floor of the firm's Euclid Avenue store.

Making the Holidays Special

(Right) RECEIVING HOLIDAY GIFTS AT JACK & HEINTZ CO., December 24, 1942

As the city of Cleveland prepared for its second Christmas Day under the blanket of World War II, on Thursday, December 24, 1942, the Jack & Heintz Company provided plant workers with some 10,000 turkeys and 5,000 food baskets. At right, Reta Kec of Macedonia receives one of the holiday turkeys from Bill Jack as other plant employees look on.

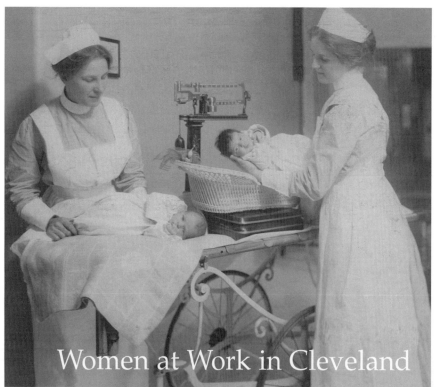

Women at Work in Cleveland

**(Left) AT ST. LUKE'S HOSPITAL
April 9, 1914**

St. Luke's Hospital was about to begin a $500,000 fund raising campaign for a new hospital when The Press published the photograph at left with a story about the campaign on Thursday, April 9, 1912. The newspaper reported, "Nurses in the maternity ward of St. Luke's Hospital are planning to make a big fight for funds when the campaign to raise $500,000 for a new hospital opens on April 14. They see at the end of the campaign a new maternity ward, equipped with the latest appliances to relieve the congestion which exists in the present quarters. With the comforts and appliances in this ward growing steadily, more and more patients are coming to the hospital. The maternity ward now is cramped for room. The weighing scales are kept busy constantly by babies who fill the ward. The infants are weighed after birth and daily till they are taken from the institution. Miss Ethel Davis (right), and Miss Catherine Sprowl (left), now have the healthiest charges. Miss Davis boasts that "Charlie"- he hasn't been officially christened yet- is the finest baby in the ward. Miss Sprowl insists "Josephine" is just as fine."

1938

1927

ANSWERING THE PHONE (Left) Women manning Ohio Bell's new automated long distance equipment in November of 1927. **(Far left)** At Ohio Bell's new switching board in 1938. **(Below)** Operators responding to the record volume of war-related long distance calls in April of 1944. In 1938, roughly 11,000 local long distance calls were recorded daily. By 1944, the number had jumped to 25,300.

1944

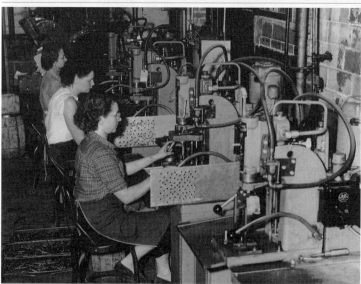

**(Left) AT LAMSON & SESSIONS CO.,
September 12, 1951**

As the Lamson & Sessions Co. prepared to mark its 85th year with a special party at Hotel Carter on Saturday, September 15, 1951, The Press published a special feature story on Wednesday, September 12th highlighting the company's rich local history. The women at left were among some 1,500 employed by the local fasteners manufacturer at their main plant at 1971 W. 85th Street and East Side facility at 913 E. 63rd Street.

(Right) THE NEW LUNCHEONETTE COUNTER AT W. T. GRANT, August 14, 1940

Cleveland's first W. T. Grant store opened at 240 Euclid Avenue on Monday, August 14, 1940. One of the features in the new store was the 117-seat luncheonette counter at right, one of two in the store, "where all glasses and dishes are sterilized and the swivel stools, all with backs, have chromium bases and are comfortably upholstered in red striped leatheret." Two opening week specials were offered- a broiled chicken dinner with a salad and au gratin potatoes or a sliced turkey plate with a salad. Complete with a roll and butter, each cost 25¢.

(Far right) AT MURRAY OHIO MFG. CO., November 9, 1946

"For the first time since the war Cleveland department stores report they have metal doll buggies, toy washing machines and toy electric irons. There are a few tubular metal swings and jungles and rubber balls and squeeze toys, and there's even an electronic game one store hopes to get in time," reported Press Industrial Editor Bertha Wellman on Saturday, November 9, 1946. Toy buyers stated, "We have more of everything," but added cautiously, "not nearly enough of anything." **(Far right)** At Murray Manufacturing Co., 115 E. 152nd St. more than 1,600 employees were turning out crimson streamlined bicycles, the first "Mercury" bikes since 1942; aluminum pursuit planes youngsters could ride in; scooters; velocipedes; wagons and the 1947 model "Zephyr" automobiles seen on the assembly line.

(Right) AT JACK & HEINTZ CO., November 11, 1943

Jack & Heintz Co. associate Miss Anna Mae Shayks (left), talks to Mrs. Ann Broth, one of nine company "goodwill ambassadors" that reported directly to Jack & Heintz Co. president Bill Jack.

(Left) OPENING THE NEW FISHER BROS. STORE ON EUCLID AVE., October 13, 1954

Thirteen-year Fisher's employee Mrs. Georgia Barlow (far left), prepares a pound of fresh ground coffee for Mrs. R. N. Sulzman during the opening of the new Fisher Bros. Master Market at 8400 Euclid Avenue on Wednesday, October 13, 1954. The store opened in Searstown East with 15,000 square feet of floor space, twice the size of the store it replaced. As part of the grand opening celebration, the first 3,000 shoppers received 29¢ bottles of Halo shampoo. Among the prizes won by shoppers were oven-ready turkeys, portable 'shoulder strap' radios, electric grill 'n wafflers and all-steel charcoal grills.

OPENING THE NEW MAY CO. STORE AT PARMATOWN MALL, August 1, 1960

"The prospect of 1,000 job openings draws scores of applicants daily to the massive four-level structure which already dominates the Parmatown skyline," reported The Press on Monday, August 1, 1960, as the May Company was in the process of hiring and training employees for its new Parmatown department store, set to open "it's ultra-modern doors" later in the month. Miss Mary Pucci, May's Parmatown employment director told The Press, "We're seeking people who will emphasize customer service, high-type people who will try to make customers feel as much at home at May's as at home." **(Right)** Trainees learn how to operate one of the store's modern cash registers from May's training director Mrs. Jacqueline Lyons (right).

Section D
Retailing in Cleveland

HIGBEE'S OPENS AT PUBLIC SQUARE,
September 8, 1931

When the Higbee Company's new Public Square store opened its doors on Tuesday, September 8, 1931, nearly 360,000 shoppers visited the store on opening day. Among the "amazing values" offered by the retailer were new fall hats for $1.39, women's silk hose for 58¢, 5,565 pairs of women's shoes for $3.94, women's wash dresses for 69¢ and men's madras print shirts for 77¢.

(Above) A doorman greets customers in front of the old Higbee Co. store on Euclid Avenue.

(Right) THE OLD HIGBEE CO. STORE AT E. 13TH, May 20, 1930

When Higbee Co. president Asa Shiverick revealed plans to build "the finest merchandising establishment in the world," a 12-story, $7,000,000, 800,000-square-foot department store as part of the new Terminal Tower complex at Public Square on Tuesday, May 20, 1930, The Press ran the photo at right of the Higbee store on Euclid Ave. at E. 13th. Shiverick's announcement dispelled rumors that Marshall Field would build on the Terminal site. The store closed its doors on Saturday, September 5, 1931, after most of its merchandise was moved to the new Public Square location.

(Below) JOHNNY ALLEN'S UNIFORM, June 13, 1938

After Tribe pitcher Johnny Allen was fined $250.00 by Cleveland Indians manager Oscar Vitt for playing in a torn shirt, a league violation, an unknown buyer purchased the shirt in question (below), and placed it on display at Higbee's downtown store on Monday, June 13, 1938. Though the purchase price and buyer were not disclosed, it was suspected that Higbee's president Charles L. Bradley, brother of Cleveland Indians owner Alva Bradley, purchased the tattered garment.

(Right) THE HIGBEE CHRISTMAS TREE, Nov. 19, 1968

The Higbee Co.'s brilliantly decorated 50-foot Christmas tree greeted visitors to the Terminal Tower foyer during the store's old fashioned holiday open house on Tuesday, November 19, 1968. Inside the department store, Mickey Mouse was on hand to greet youngsters.

Linder Coy

(Left) THE NEW LINDER COY STORE ON EUCLID AT E. 14TH, 1915

When Linder Coy opened its new department store at Euclid Avenue and E. 14th St. on Monday, September 13, 1915, the store's newspaper ad proclaimed, "What the architects have done in creating a building of distinct individuality and artistic character, our merchandising organization has endeavored to accomplish within these walls, a gathering of entirely new Fashionable Feminine Apparel quite as unique, original and artistic as the building itself." The new store, under construction at left, opened at 10 A.M. with its first-floor women's hat shop selling tailored hats for $5 and its women's suit shop offering fur-trimmed broadcloth suits for $19.50. On the fourth floor was the store's Hair Dressing and Manicuring Shop and a Tea Shop ideal for luncheons and afternoon tea.

(Below) THE NEW STERLING LINDER, 1949

On Friday, March 11, 1949, the Sterling & Welch Co. was acquired by New York-based Allied Stores Corp., which already owned the W. B. Davis Co. and Lindner's. Below, work is underway to combine the W. B. Davis and Linder stores into one unit. The new store opened on Monday, August 1, 1949. On Friday, June, 1950, the Sterling & Welch Co. and Linder-Davis Co. stores were merged to form Sterling, Linder-Davis Co.

Sterling, Linder Davis Co.

Sterling & Welch Co.

(Above) THE MERRY-GO-ROUND, December 13, 1949

"The magic of Christmas shone in the faces of these tots who braved blustery winds to go downtown for an interview with Santa Claus and a preview of toy department offerings," offered The Press on Tuesday, December 13, 1949, as the colorful merry-go-round above awaited youngsters at Sterling & Welch Co.

(Right) THE STERLING LINDER-DAVIS CHRISTMAS TREE, November 27, 1956

"The great Christmas tree at Sterling Linder-Davis (at right), tallest indoor tree in America, is installed and ready for the 150,000 visitors who annually come from a dozen states to see it," reported The Press on Tuesday, November 27, 1956, as downtown retailers welcomed holiday shoppers with only 23 shopping days remaining. The department store's annual Christmas tree display can be traced back to the early 1930's.

(Left) EASTER SHOPPING, March 26, 1932

Local weatherman G. Harold Noyes predicted colder weather for Easter Sunday with the probability of rain, possibly changing to snow flurries, as the shoppers at left completed their Easter shopping on Saturday, March 26, 1932. While fur coats were expected to be "the outstanding style note," Press reporter Helen N. Allyn wrote, "Mlady's Easter bonnet can wear flowers this year, but in most instances will prefer a neat tailored ribbon bow. It will probably have a slight brim tilted over her right eye, or it might be a close-fitting turban sporting a nose veil over mysterious eyes." Allyn added, "Florists say quality, rather than quantity is the secret of the smart corsage this year. One or two orchids or a discreet cluster of gardenias for shoulder wear." Among the crowds expected to attend the pontifical Mass in St. John Cathedral or Easter services at Trinity Episcopal Cathedral would be men, "carrying lightweight malacca sticks and wearing light gray spats over patent-leather oxfords," according to Allyn.

The May Company

(Above) HOLIDAY SHOPPING, Nov. 26, 1954

As shoppers passed the May Co. on Friday, November 26, 1954, inside, store specials included Nyla-Gab Storm Coats for $12.00; Orlon Cardigans for $4.99; men's Dacron "no fade" sports shirts for $2.99; "Baby Bunting" dolls for $8.88 and 21-inch Artone console T.V.'s for $169.00.

(Right) THE MAY CO. CELEBRATES 50 YEARS, October 5, 1949

Women's all-wool sweaters, originally $5.00 to $6.00 were priced at $3.69 and $4.69; new fall felt hats regularly $7.50 to $10.00 were reduced to $5.50, and a Westinghouse Radio-Phonograph console regularly $189.95 was marked down to $95.00, during the May Company's 50th anniversary sale on Wednesday, October 5, 1949. After ten additions to the retailer's headquarters at Public Square (right), the store was reported to be Ohio's largest retail outlet.

COLLEEN MOORE'S DOLL HOUSE, July 16, 1935

The "world's loveliest doll house" came to the May Co. on Wednesday, July 16, 1935, as motion picture star Colleen Moore's fourteen-foot high, $435,000 doll house, complete with electricity and running water, was placed on display for a two-week period in the department store's 3rd floor auditorium. A newspaper ad describing the miniature showpiece offered, "See the great entrance hall with its fantastic stairway, look down at onyx floors, at pillars finished in gold, the tiny yet perfect pieces of furniture and bric-a-brac." Over 2,000 tiny objects of furnishings, with rich jewels and precious metals, floors inlaid with gold and silver, miniature books hand-written by noted authors and a diamond-hung chandelier lit by light bulbs no larger than grains of wheat, were featured in the exquisite doll house. The admittance fee of 10¢ for children and 20¢ for adults was donated to local hospitals for crippled children.

Wm. Taylor & Sons

(Left) SHOPPING AT TAYLOR'S, September 22, 1934

One department store exclaimed, "looks like a record," while another offered, "big increase yesterday over last year and a big increase today over yesterday," on Saturday, September 22, 1934, as the city's annual carnival of bargains entered its second day. At left, shoppers fight traffic to reach Wm. Taylor & Sons for some bargain hunting.

(Below left) TAYLOR'S NEW ESCALATORS, July 16, 1946

Wm. Taylor Son & Co. employees, below left, got ready for their first ride on the department store's newly-installed escalator system on Monday, July 16, 1946, as David Scholl, vice president and general manager, started the store's new people mover. To celebrate the occasion, store employees arrived early to ride the new system while enjoying free coffee and doughnuts. When completed, the escalator was set to run from the basement to the eighth floor and have a capacity of 1,600 people at one time. At the time, the escalator system was completed to the third floor.

(Left) TAYLOR'S BIRTHDAY PARTY, October 24, 1941

Wm. Taylor Co. employees and officials celebrated the store's 26th birthday at Hotel Hollenden on Friday, October 24, 1941.

(Right) BUYING DEFENSE STAMPS AND BONDS, February 19, 1942

Onlookers braved near zero temperatures to witness the opening of Taylor's new Defense Stamp and Bond Station in their downtown store's huge front window on Thursday, February 19, 1942. At right, Auxiliary Bishop James A. McFadden purchases the first stamp from Mrs. C. J. Carlin and Mrs. Farrell Gallagher representing the Cleveland Diocesan Council of the National Council of Catholic Women, one of the area groups called on to volunteer at the makeshift station, created by installing doors in place of two large glass window panels.

The Bailey Company

(Right) BAILEY'S AT ONTARIO & PROSPECT, April 29, 1949

As the department store marked its 50th year of servicing customers from its downtown store at Prospect and Ontario (at right), on Friday, April 29, 1949, Bailey's president Lambert G. Oppenheim told The Press, "This business was founded on the Golden Rule. We operate this rule three ways. We treat our customers as we'd like them to treat us. We are fair and reasonable with the people who supply us, and they treat us the same way. We do unto employees as we'd like them to do unto us. I think it makes for a happy family here." During its anniversary celebration, Bailey's provided a special buying service on Sunday offering patrons the chance to shop from home by calling Cherry 3820 from 10 A.M. to 4 P.M. That weekend, Bailey's offered communion frocks for $6.95 and $8.95; a 3-piece modern sectional sofa, regularly $125.00 for $25 each piece; better women's coats in three styles for only $38.00 and stylish Smartleigh worsted men's suits for $45.00, most with extra trousers only $14.95. The local landmark was demolished in the summer of 1963 to make way for a 13-story parking garage.

(Right) BAILEY'S EMPLOYEE PARTY, May 6, 1936

"Youth entertained age last night when the Bailey Co. entertained 820 employees in the Rainbow Room of Hotel Carter," reported The Press on Thursday, May 7, 1936. At right, Bailey Co. employees enjoying the party.

(Right) BUYING THE FIRST POSTWAR NYLONS, January 3, 1946

After thousands of area women stormed downtown stores to get the first postwar nylon stockings on 'N-Day,' Thursday, January 3, 1946, The Press reported, "Bells rang, doors opened, barriers went down and with whoopees that caused office workers to pause in their labors and take a look-see, the lines of people disappeared into the stores like strings of spaghetti sucked in by children." Minutes after the doors were opened, the crowds at right jammed the nylon counter at Bailey's where purchases were limited to a single pair per customer. One elated store patron beamed, "This is the nicest thing that's happened to me since my son came home from overseas." A couple of young females, when asked to be photographed wearing the nylons, refused stating, "Na, we can't. You see we work at another department store, but missed out on getting them there. So we had to come here."

(Left) AT THE PERFUME COUNTER, December 24, 1931

As the shoppers at left picked up last-minute gifts at Halle's perfume counter, The Press reported on Thursday, December 24, 1931, "Perfume counters were doing a brisk volume of business today as the men finally got around to do their Christmas shopping."

(Below) AT THE PERFUME COUNTER, December 24, 1953

Men's wool and cashmere mufflers were priced at $7.50 at Halle's Treasure House of Gifts, when the photograph below of last minute shopper John MacArthur with foot-weary Miss Shirley Bryan at Halle's perfume counter appeared on the front page of The Press on Thursday, December 24, 1953.

Halle Brothers Company

(Right) PRINCE MATCHABELLI

During a lecture at Halle's on Thursday, November 24, 1934, Prince Georges Matchabelli (right), remarked, "A flower without its scent is the woman without perfume. Glamour mystery, allure- the qualities most desired by women- are not captured by a smart hat or the latest model frock, but the aromatic odor of a fragrant perfume."

(Below) HALLE COMPANY MANAGEMENT, Aug. 1, 1949

When Halle's climaxed a three-year, $10,000,000 expansion program with the opening of the first floor of its new

air-conditioned west wing on Monday, August 1, 1947, senior store management included A. E. Jacques, vice president and general merchandise manager (left); 81-year-old chairman of the board Samuel H. Halle; 44-year-old president Walter M. Halle; J. Henry Dippel, vice president and general superintendent; Jay I. Glaser, executive vice president and controller; and board of directors member Herbert S. Moorehouse (right).

(Right) LUCILLE BALL VISITS HALLE'S, January 31, 1956

On Tuesday, January 31, 1956, Lucille Ball and husband Desi Arnaz arrived in Cleveland during a 17-day, 10-city nationwide tour to promote their new movie "Forever Darling," set to open at Loew's State on Playhouse Square, Wednesday, February 8, 1956. After taking part in a Heart Fund rally at Hotel Statler, Lucy (center right), took time out to visit the toy department at Halle's in search of presents for her two children, Lucy and 3-year-old Desi IV. At the time, her hit show, "I Love Lucy," which aired Monday nights at 9 P.M. on WXEL-Channel 8, was the second most popular show on television. Their new movie, produced by Zanra (Arnaz spelled backwards) Productions, starred Lucy, Desi and James Mason as Lucy's guardian angel. The celebrated couple traveled the country in a plush private railroad car complete with Lucy's own hairdresser and maid.

Rock Hudson Comes to Halle's

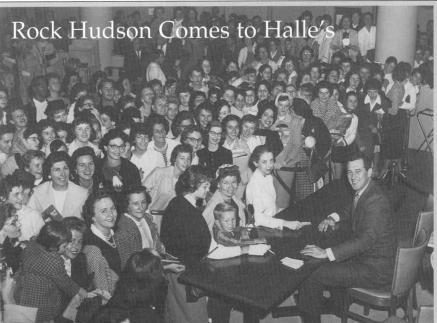

October 9, 1959

The newspaper advertisement on Friday, October 9, 1959 offered, "See the Stars (and producer) of "Pillow Talk" on Stage! In Person- 10:00 p.m. Tonight- Gala Premiere Showing," as the Hippodrome Theater at 720 Euclid Avenue prepared for the Midwest premiere that evening of "Pillow Talk," starring Rock Hudson and Doris Day. Bill Gordon served as master of ceremonies as Hudson, supporting actress Thelma Ritter and the movie's producer, Ross Hunter, appeared at the Hippodrome to welcome movie goers before the show. Prior to his premiere appearance, Hudson was greeted by over 250 young women at a special afternoon autograph session sponsored by Halle's (above). The Press noted that when Hudson entered the department store's Tea Room, "Although the women were mainly teenagers, there was no screaming, just one big sigh as Rock showed up to sign "Pillow Talk" records." Following the autograph session, Hudson attended a reception at Statler Hotel for media and movie people before heading to the Hippodrome.

Section E
Entertainment

At Euclid Beach Park

"When I came back in 1920, there weren't many rides, head mechanic Walter Williams told Press reporter Mary Swindell. "But one by one, all these rides were added, and I worked on every one of them. The Laff-in-the-Dark, The Thriller, Over the Falls, Flying Scooters.... It takes a long time to build up an amusement park. Unless you're Walt Disney, you can't do it overnight." Williams made his remarks only days before Euclid Beach Park, the popular lakefront attraction famous for its rollercoasters and popcorn balls, closed its doors on Sunday September 28, 1969, after 73 years of operation.

Cleveland's Palace Theater on Playhouse Square featured the swing sounds of Jimmy Dorsey and his orchestra on Friday, April 21, 1939, while next door, 16-year-old MGM singing sensation Judy Garland headlined the first vaudeville presentation at Loew's State in three years. Appearing here for the first time, Garland was touring between pictures following the release of "Listen, Darling." Her next film opened locally at Loew's State on Friday, August 18, 1939. It was MGM's spectacular technicolor triumph, "The Wizard of Oz," with Cleveland actress Margaret Hamilton playing Miss Gulch, the "Wicked Witch of the West."

(Right) Before performing at the State that evening, the talented starlet was invited by Cleveland Indians president Alva Bradley to sing "The Star Spangled Banner," during pre-game ceremonies at Municipal Stadium as the Indians opened the 1939 season. At right, Judy is joined before the game by Bradley (left), Mayor Harold H. Burton, who threw out the first pitch, and Tribe skipper Oscar Vitt.

(Below) Judy Garland delivers "The Star Spangled Banner," before 23,957 rather frigid Opening Day fans. Cleveland beat starter Harry Eisenstat and Detroit Tigers, 5-1, as young ace right-hander Bob Feller, who struck out ten, pitched a complete-game, three-hitter for the win.

Friday, April 21, 1939
Judy Garland Sings at the Indians' Home Opener

STARTING LINEUPS

CLEVELAND	DETROIT
Skeeter Webb ss	Barney McCosky cf
Ben Chapman cf	Fred Walker lf
Earl Averill rf	Charlie Gehringer 2b
Jeff Heath lf	Hank Greenberg 1b
Hal Trosky 1b	Rudy York c
Ken Keltner 3b	Pete Fox rf
Frankie Pytlak c	Bill Rogell 3b
Jim Shilling 2b	Frank Croucher ss
Bob Feller p	Harry Eisenstat p

(Left, Below) GEORGE JESSEL STARS IN "THE JAZZ SINGER" AT THE OHIO THEATER, February 6, 1927

Billed as "America's foremost young actor," vaudeville comic George Jessel opened in "The Jazz Singer" at Ohio Theater on Sunday, February 6, 1927. On Wednesday, February 9th, The Press reported that Jessel had asked the paper to help him find eight chorus girls for a rehearsal scene. When he arrived at the theater, Jessel was surprised to find nearly 200 young lovelies waiting for the tryout. Seeing "the number of good-looking, shapely girls in Cleveland," he decided he wanted 10 for the scene. At far left, Jessel (on the piano), is surrounded by eight of the local beauties. Matinee tickets for "The Jazz Singer" were priced from 50¢ to $2.00 during its two-week stay.

(Right) YO-YOS AND AUNT JEMIMA, June 18, 1930

"The yo-yo craze almost cost Aunt Jemima (at right), a pink ticket yesterday," reported The Press on Wednesday, June 18, 1930. "On her way out of the R-K-O Palace Theater after her performance, Herb Smith, "yo-yo" expert, handed her one of the tiny discs. She sat in her car so long trying to figure out different tricks with her yo-yo, that Mark Hanna traffic patrolman, was going to give her a ticket." Aunt Jemima, the "late star of Ziegfeld's Show Boat," was performing as part of a vaudeville slate at B. F. Keith's refrigerated Palace Theatre "Cleveland's Favorite Summer Resort" on Playhouse Square. At the time, The Press and the Palace Theater were teaming up to offer the addicting toys, popular in the south, to Clevelanders for free.

Playhouse Square: The Theatre Heart of Cleveland

(Left) OUR GANG AT THE STATE, Sept. 1, 1928

After arriving in town for a week's engagement at Loew's State on Playhouse Square, the six members of Hal Roach's Hollywood troupe "Our Gang," were introduced to over 1,000 area orphans in the theater's lobby during a special morning show sponsored by the theater and The Press on Saturday, September 1, 1928. On stage left to right are "Wheezer;" "Farina;" Joe Cobb, "the fat boy;" Mary Ann Jackson, "the tiny miss with the dimples;" Jean Darling, "the cute little girl" and Harry Spear, "Freckles." Hidden from sight was Pete the dog. The orphans were transported to the State in 27 busses furnished by the Cleveland Railway Co.

(Right)
MEETING HOLLYWOOD STARS AT LOEW'S STATE, November 25, 1959

Over sixty students and teachers representing local dramatics clubs and classes from 25 area high schools met with Hollywood performers (left to right), Lita Baron (Mrs. Calhoun), Rory Calhoun, Rhonda Fleming, Louis Jordan and John Agar in the lobby of Loew's State for a question and answer session on Friday, November 25, 1959. During the informal actor-to-actor chat, one of the students asked Rhonda Fleming how it was to work with Bing Crosby and Bob Hope. Fleming replied, "I learned to laugh at myself. Bing told me once, 'Stop worrying Fleming, You don't have very much to do in the picture anyway'." The stars were performing in the week-long engagement of David O. Selnick's gala stage show, "Hollywood Stars" at the State.

Tom Hanks- A Great Lakes Shakespeare Festival Alumnus

1978

1977

The largest acting company assembled in Great Lakes Shakespeare Festival (GLSF) history opened the festival's new season at Lakewood Civic Auditorium in July of 1978. Joining veterans Bairbre Dowling, Sara Woods, actor-director Vincent Dowling, Bernard Kates, Norm Berman, Dennis Lipscomb, George Maguire, Michael John McGann, Holmes Osborn and Edith Owen, were six new members, Jon Peter Benson, Donna Emmanuel, Tom Blair, Richard Dix, Frederic-Winslow Oram and Tom Hanks (above). Hanks had been studying in California after serving as an GLSF intern in 1977. The musical "Polly" opened the GLSF season on Friday, July 7th, with Emmanuel in the title role.

(Above right) Hanks with Bert Goldstein during his GLSF internship in 1977. The two men were performing in "Taming of the Shrew."

(Right) Directed by Vincent Dowling, "Do Me A Favorite" opened as part of the Great Lakes Shakespeare Festival at Lakewood Civic Auditorium on Friday, July 26, 1979. At right, Hanks rehearses as Henry V in "Do Me" with Mary Kay Dean, who played Katherine. Also in the cast were Jody Catlin, Robert Elliott and Clive Rosengren.

1979

Headlining The Cleveland Press Christmas Charity Show

(Left) ERROL FLYNN, December 9, 1940

A concert by the Wurlitzer Band at 7:30 P.M. began the night's entertainment, as a record turnout of over 18,000 came out to see handsome Warner Brothers star Errol Flynn (at left with Shirley Hurlbert), headline the sixth annual Press Christmas Charity Show at Public Hall on Monday, December 9, 1940. Richard Endress, who imitated Ted Lewis, won the amateur contest. Flynn's appearance produced the largest local indoor crowd to attend a single entertainment event at the time.

(Below) ABBOTT & COSTELLO, November 18, 1941

Over 15,000 paid from 30¢ to $1.10 to see Lou Costello (left), and Bud Abbott, stars of the upcoming movie "Keep "Em Flying," headline the seventh annual Press Christmas Fund Show at Public Hall on Tuesday, November 18, 1941. Also performing that night were the 120-piece Wurlitzer band, Lee Gordon's 12-piece WTAM Radio orchestra and 26 amateur acts. 13-year-old pianist Joe Hlavacek won the top prize.

(Lower right) DANNY KAYE, November 23, 1946

Danny Kaye fans began standing in line at 5:45 A.M. on November 11, 1946, for tickets to the 12th annual Press Christmas Charity Show at Public Hall on Saturday, November 23, 1946. A standing room crowd of over 12,000 paid either 90¢, $1.25 or $1.80 to see Kaye, "the wonder man of screen and radio." During the show, Press Editor Louis B. Seltzer presented Kaye an RCA table model television set inscribed above "the vision screen" with, "In sincere appreciation to Danny Kaye from The Press Christmas Show, 1946. Thanks, Cleveland, Ohio." Fourteen-year-old Richard Melari of Lincoln Junior High School won the amateur competition and the $100 first prize, with imitations of Bob Eberle, Vaughn Monroe and Frank Sinatra. Winning $50 for finishing second was the Ukrainian Dancing Guild group led by Andrew Boyko. At far right, Kaye attempts a "Ukrainian squat-dance," during the show.

(Right) Buying tickets for the Danny Kaye show in The Cleveland Press Building lobby.

(Left) JIMMY STEWART, December 17, 1947

Popular entertainer Jimmy Stewart rehearses before serving as master of ceremonies at the 13th annual Cleveland Press Christmas Charity Show on Wednesday, December 17, 1947. Over 8,500 watched the Public Hall program where Ray Aiello, 16, and Ray Evans, 17, captured top amateur honors. During the show Press Editor Louis B. Seltzer presented Stewart with a bag of golf clubs. The annual Press event was honored by becoming part of WEWS-TV's inaugural night of broadcasting.

November 1st & 2nd 1953, The Press Celebrates 75 Years

November 1st

(Above) RCA-Victor star Eddie Fisher wows the audience of 6,000 at Cleveland Arena during "The Press Jubilee Hit Tune Party," on Sunday, November 1st. Joining Fisher were Decca recording star Pat Morissey, Buddy Greco, Kitty Kallen and emcees Howie Lund, Phil McLean, Joe Mulvihill and Johnny Andrews. **(Above right)** Eddie Fisher signs the music of opera star Mildred Miller.

November 2nd

(Above) Comedian George Jessel, who served as master of ceremonies, posed with singers from Ray Anthony's band during The Press "Salute to Cleveland" show on Monday, November 2nd. The "Salute" show climaxed a three-night festival of special events that began with a Golden Wedding Party at Public Hall on Saturday night. Over 30 entertainers were involved in the anniversary shows including Tommy Edwards, Jackie Lynn, Bonnie Lou, Henry (Hot Lips) Levine and Glenn Rowell.

(Above right)
Featured during the "Salute to Cleveland" show were Clevelanders pianist Arthur Loesser, (left), opera star Mildred Miller, trumpeter Ray Anthony, accordionist Sal Bucarey and Hollywood actor Jim Backus (right). More than 7,000 came out to Public Hall for the free night of music, singing and dancing.

(Left) As trumpeter Ray Anthony and his band marched through the Public Hall audience playing, "When the Saints Come Marching In," Jessel grabbed a clarinet and began mocking the performers. Others performing that evening included Eddie Fisher, Bernice Parks, the George Shearing Quintet, the Wonder and Banks dance team, baritone Robert Weede and Richard Hayman.

(Left) ARTUR RODZINSKI ARRIVES, October 6, 1933

Prior to making his Severance Hall debut on Thursday, October 26, 1933, Dr. Artur Rodzinski, the orchestra's new musical director, met with members of the women's committee of the Cleveland Orchestra on Friday, October 6, 1933. At left, Rodzinski, who succeeded Nikolai Sokoloff, the orchestra's original conductor, is seen shaking hands with Mrs. Charles H. Strong.

(Far left below) JASCHA HEIFETZ, December 4, 1939

Famed violinist Jascha Heifetz (left), was joined by his accompanist Emanuel Bay and Dr. Artur Rodzinski (right), on Monday, December 4, 1939, in preparation for concerts at Severance Hall on Thursday, December 7, and Saturday, December 9, 1939.

Musical Mastery- The Cleveland Orchestra

(Left) GEORGE SZELL & BRUNO WALTER, March 9, 1950

Press music critic Arthur Loesser wrote, "It was an immediate experience of cultural continuity, of direct union with the spirit and genius of the past," after celebrated German conductor Bruno Walter led the Cleveland Orchestra in Mahler's First Symphony at Severance Hall on Thursday, March 9, 1950. At left, Walter (right), dined with George Szell after arriving here for his guest appearance.

George Szell Begins his Tenure with the Cleveland Orchestra, October 17, 1946

(Left)

Internationally acclaimed conductor George Szell (center), who accepted a three-year appointment to succeed Erich Leinsdorf as musical director of the Cleveland Orchestra on January, 24, 1946, posed with the orchestra in full dress prior to his Severance Hall debut on Thursday, October 17, 1946. Press Critic Milton Widder called Szell's appointment, "One of the best-heralded events in the city's musical history."

(Right) EUNICE PODIS, June 1, 1954

Popular local pianist Eunice Podis, "Miss Pops," rehearses with guest conductor Andre Kostelanetz on June 1, 1954 for her upcoming pops concert performance of Tchaikovsky's First Piano Concerto with the 71-piece Cleveland Orchestra ensemble on Saturday, June 12th. Tickets for the Public Hall concert ranged from 50¢ to $2.00.

(Far right) LOUIS LANE WITH DUKE ELLINGTON, June 28, 1961

Cleveland Summer orchestra conductor Louis Lane (left), rehearses with jazz legend Duke Ellington before their Public Hall Pops Concert on Wednesday, June 28, 1961. Ellington's 15-piece band joined the orchestra in performing such favorites as "Mood Indigo," and "Sophisticated Lady." Tickets ranged from 75¢ to $3.00.

(Right) ARTHUR RUBENSTEIN, March 29, 1976

"There was evident fondness and respect for the genius of this remarkable, young 90-year-old on the part of the orchestra and conductor Maazel," wrote Press Music Critic Frank Hruby, after celebrated pianist Arthur Rubenstein (at right), performed before a "standing, cheering, whistling SRO crowd," at Severance Hall on Monday, March 29, 1976.

"Even if your dream machine spins out the birthday party of the year, it couldn't come close to the celebration 2,000 happy people shared with the Cleveland Orchestra last night at Severance Hall," wrote Press Society Editor Marjorie Alge, after the Cleveland Orchestra, under the direction of Lorin Maazel (at podium right), celebrated its 60th anniversary with a special concert on Sunday, December 10, 1978. The festive night featured several pieces performed during the orchestra's original concert at Grays Armory in 1918, along with radiant performances by soprano Beverly Sills, a Cleveland native (at right and above), and famed violinist Isaac Stern. During the concert, Maazel stepped to the piano where he joined Sills and Stern in singing "Happy Birthday Cleveland Orchestra."

The Cleveland Orchestra Celebrates 60 Years,
December 10, 1978

The 1936 Great Lakes Exposition

On Saturday, June 27, 1936, Cleveland's memorable Great Lakes Exposition opened amid the fanfare of ribbon-snipping, military music and fireworks. First envisioned by Lincoln Dickey and fostered under the corporate leadership of Dudley Blossom, the $25 million, 135-acre fantasyland opened exactly 80 days after ground-breaking ceremonies. At 9 P.M. that evening, auto maker Henry Ford pushed a button in Dearborn, Michigan to formally dedicate the Parade of Years, one of the main Expo areas. The first night ended with fireworks shot from a barge in Lake Erie. Over 8,000 visitors traveled through the turnstiles on Opening Day, the first of nearly four million spectators visiting the civic wonderland during its 108-day run.

(Left) An aerial view of the Great Lakes Exposition which stretched almost a mile along the lakefront from Municipal Stadium to roughly E. 19th Street. The two structures immediately east of the Stadium are the Hall of Progress (foreground), and the Automotive Building.

(Left) Shown during the very busy Labor Day weekend, the art deco Court of Presidents, a main Expo entrance, linked the upper mall level where a number of event attractions such as the Sherwin-Williams orchestra shell were located, to the lower level along the lakefront. The Great Lakes Exposition was created to celebrate the 100th anniversary of Cleveland's incorporation as a city.

(Right) As a crowd of some 5,000 gathered to be the first inside the lakefront wonderland, Miss Marguerite Bacon (center), cut a multi-colored ribbon at noon to open the Great Lakes Exposition on the 27th. Bacon, the great-great-great great-granddaughter of General Moses Cleaveland, cut the ribbon after President Franklin D. Roosevelt, pushed a button from Washington D. C., which triggered a large bell atop one of the Expo entrances. The fair grounds' elaborate night-lighting scheme, designed in part by General Electric's Nela Park, used enough light each evening to light a city of 45,000.

(Left) The Lakeside Avenue entrance to the Exposition grounds just prior to opening day in 1936. To the left in front of the Court House is the Brick House with an interior designed by the Bailey Co. Immediately behind the brick house is the Lumber House with an interior designed by the Halle Bros. Co. Fifteen miles of paved streets and walkways stretched through the Exposition grounds. Eddie Cantor, Fibber McGee and Molly, and Paul Whiteman were among the famous entertainers performing at the Expo.

One of the most popular attractions at the Great Lakes Exposition was the "Marine Theater" located immediately northeast of Municipal Stadium. Free shows were held daily, most filled to capacity, featuring a variety of aquatic performers including fifty of the area's best high school swimmers, 280-pound cannonballer "Tiny" Gorman and P. J. Ringens, who plunged 125 feet into Lake Erie. Below right, eleven divers perform one of several synchronized routines to music provided by Merle Jacobs' orchestra. A powerboat display along the lakefront climaxed each show. When the Expo opened for a second season in 1937, the Marine Theater had been replaced by a lavish Aquacade under the direction of celebrated producer Billy Rose. Johnny Weismuller of Tarzan fame and Eleanor Holmes Jarrett were two of the featured Aquacade performers.

The Marine Theater

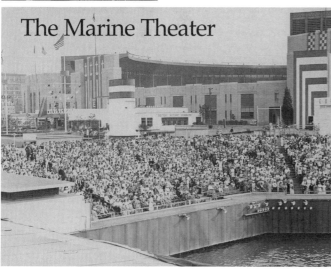

The French Casino

When the Great Lakes Exposition opened on Monday, June 28, 1936, a newspaper ad for "Folies du Nuit" at the French Casino in the Expo's Streets of the World exclaimed, "You should see it twice- You must see in Once. Never before such a show. Everything you have seen pales into significance beside it. Now you must see "Vision Nude" and the bevy of callipygian beauties. What you get at the French Casino! A complete show of exotic swing, daring conception... Dancing to two outstanding orchestras, Johnny Huntington and Tom Flynn. Fine food and drink in one of America's most beautiful cafes." On the same day, a newspaper story offered the following account, "The French Casino, which is rapidly gaining notoriety as the "hot spot" of the Great Lakes Exposition yesterday completed its second day of entertainment without formal complaint being lodged, but was given an unofficial visit by two policemen from Central Station last night. The policemen "just stopped in to make a phone call," while strolling through the Streets of the World. It so happened that one of the highly talked-of floor shows was in progress. Leaving at the conclusion of the show and carrying detailed, illustrated programs, they commented: We saw nothing

here that anyone should complain of- if he paid come here to witness it. However, they did expect complaints to be made, they said."

(Left, Above) Next to the French Casino was the Nudist Colony, one of 490 different buildings crowded into the Streets of the World. (Top right) The infamous Toto La Verne, one of the "Vision Nudes." (Above) During a training session at the French Casino.

(Left) Rainy weather did not stop the youngsters at left, who were among the thousands of area children participating in The Press National Marble Tourney Finals and Junior Balloon Race at Euclid Beach on Saturday, June 7, 1931. Prizes of $5, $3 and $2 were distributed to the owners, and finders, of the balloons traveling the greatest distance after being released. Edward Kovac of Euclid won an all-expense paid trip to the national marbles tournament in Ocean City, New Jersey, after beating 30 silver medal winners to capture the Euclid Beach tourney.

(Left, Far left) Over 2,500 youngsters from 16 area children's homes, including the youngsters far left and the two cute 5-year-olds at left, enjoyed "a big spree from the merry-go-round to chute-the-chutes and popcorn and peanuts and candy cane," during the American Automobile Club's annual youth outing at Euclid Beach on Tuesday, July 2, 1957.

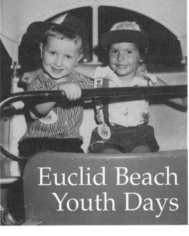

Euclid Beach Youth Days

(Below, Below left) Entertained throughout the day by a number of local celebrities including Mayor Anthony J. Celebreeze (below), and Cleveland Browns star Lou "The Toe" Groza (below left), over 2,600 youngsters participated in the Cleveland Automobile Club's annual youth day outing at Euclid Beach on Thursday, July 7, 1960. Joining the rides and free gifts in popularity were the park's concession stands, where happy youngsters consumed an estimated one and a quarter miles of hot dogs, while satisfying their sweet tooth on ice cream and the park's popular pop corn balls.

(Left, Below left) **May 25, 1953** "King Jack reigned supreme when it came to handing out free Liberty Ice Cream's and Howdy Dowdy twin pops during "The Press-Red Feather Puritas Springs Park Day" Saturday afternoon," reported The Press on Monday, May 25, 1953. More than 1,000 youngsters from Community Fund agencies, including the ones receiving freezer treats and waiting in line for the Moon Rocket below left, attended the free day of summertime fun as guests of park management and Press Sights and Sounds editor Milton Widder.

Puritas Springs Park

(Right) "From "flea-hoppers" to the more graceful exponents of the circle waltz, the roller rink at Puritas Park (right), has long been a popular stamping ground for local skating enthusiasts," wrote Press reporter Dan Chabek on Friday, July 10, 1942. Chabek's article was the 10th in a series of Press stories on wartime summer outings with special emphasis on tire and gas economy. "For a number of years the park's famed Cyclone Coaster has laid a claim as undisputed sectional champ among roller coasters and one of the world's highest. Fortified with an armful of first-hand impressions from an afternoon visit to this park, overlooking Rocky River Valley at Grayton and Puritas Springs road, we know of some pretty good reasons for acquainting yourself with the park this season," Chabek reported. One of the unusual attractions Chabek pointed to was the park's new Moon Rocket, one of the few rides added locally in 1942. "Revolving at 60 miles an hour around a huge disk 40 feet in diameter, the Moon Rocket was the amusement industry's latest contrivance in thrills and has its biggest following in the evenings when a play of lights adds to the flying-through space sensation," the reporter revealed.

(Right) **July, 1940** A summer outing at Puritas Springs Park in July of 1940. Part of the Cyclone rollercoaster can be seen behind the park patrons.

Section F
Radio & TV

WTAM RADIO, 1928

After hearing through the Cleveland Chamber of Commerce that the Willard Storage Battery Co. would either sell or close local radio stations WTAM and WEAR, the Van Sweringen interests and the Cleveland Electric Illuminating Co. took over operation of the two stations on Thursday, May 31, 1928. "The stations will be continued at the location in The Union Trust Building in Chester avenue and the executive and operating personnel will not be changed," reported The Press on Wednesday, May 30, 1928. The Illuminating Company issued a statement that added, "Recognizing the fact that this radio station is a civic asset to the Greater Cleveland district and that the cessation of its operation would be a real loss, the Van Sweringen interests and the Illuminating Co. entered into arrangements to continue it. Every effort will be made to maintain the station on a plane which will make it of maximum value to the community."

(Below) NEW WJW DJ SOUPY HINES (Soupy Sales), April 27, 1951

On Friday, April 27, 1951, veteran Press reporter Stan Anderson wrote in his 'See-Hear with Stan Anderson' column, "Soupy Hines (below), WJW's new disc jockey is glad the weather is getting warmer. He has scarcely anything but underwear in his wardrobe. His first night in town he stayed at the YMCA and parked his car nearby. Somebody broke into the car and made away with $350 worth of clothes. Left with a pair of slacks and a sports jacket, Soupy is now waiting for his first paycheck. If he doesn't get it soon, he will have to work in his long undies. His shows are heard daily at 6 A.M. and 3:30 P.M." While Soupy's morning show aired against Bill

Mayer on WGAR, Tom Haley on WTAM, Walt Kay on WDOK and Bill Gordon on WHK; he competed in the afternoon with Bill Randle on WERE and House Party and Arthur Godfrey on WGAR. On local television at 3:30 P.M. was "Remember This" on WNBK-Channel 4; "Women's Window" on WEWS-Channel 5; and "Betty Crocker" on WXEL-Channel 9.

Radio Days

(Left) JOE FINAN, October 1, 1955

Starting on October 1, 1955, popular WJW 850 DJ Joe Finan (left), made daily appearances at the five-day Cleveland Press "Do-It-Yourself, Photo and Hobby Show." Finan emceed Coke parties from 4 to 6 P.M. each day for teenagers who received tickets from their school's Press High-Time correspondents.

(Right) WGAR GREASERS, 1973

"These WGAR air personalities- who look like they might be thinking of stealing the hub caps off the 1957 Thunderbird they surround- will host a gigantic sock hop at Richmond Mall Tuesday night at 6:30," announced The Press in its "In" section on Friday, July 6, 1973. In front are Joe Mayer (left), John Lanigan, Loren Owens, Geoff Fox and Chuck Collier. Standing behind the Thunderbird are Chick Watkins, Brian Beirne, Jim Buchanan and Buddy Henderson. "Wildflower" provided music at the event which coincided with a special screening of "Let The Good Times Roll," at Loew's East I.

THE WTAM RADIO MORNING BANDWAGON, November 2, 1953

WTAM Radio joined The Press in celebrating the paper's 75th anniversary on Monday, November 2, 1953, with a special two-hour tribute during its "Morning Bandwagon" show. Singer-pianist Johnny Andrews (below right), vocalist Jackie Lynn and Henry 'Hot Lips' Levine (center), joined the 17-piece WTAM orchestra in a number of musical salutes including "Get Your Papers," the first hit song for popular singer Eddie Fisher, who was headlining The Press "Salute to Cleveland" show that evening at Public Hall.

(Below right) Press Editor Louis B. Seltzer (second, left), is joined at the birthday cake on November 2nd by WTAM-WNBK General Manager Lloyd E. Yoder (left), and Bandwagon stars Johnny Andrews, Henry Levine and Jackie Lynn.

(Left) BILL RANDLE WITH ANNA MARIA ALBERGHETTI, December 21, 1957

After interviewing the celebrated starlet at left, WJW-Radio DJ Bill Randle wrote in his "Randle on Record" column in the Home section of The Press on Saturday, December 21, 1957, "The concert stage had given us recently a tremendously talented young lady whose career began at the age of six in Italy. Her name is Anna Maria Alberghetti. Anna Marie is now 21. She is a beautiful and talented girl with a full-fledged career in movies, TV, records and the concert stage. The wonderful thing about Anna Maria Alberghetti is that she is not only talented, but is a wholesome, sparkling personality."

(Below left) BROADCASTING LIVE September 23, 1959

Battling for local listenership on Wednesday, September 23, 1959, KYW 1100 AM disc jockeys broadcast around the clock from the mobile van in front of the station's studios at 815 Superior Ave. As morning jock Big Wilson delivered his show on top of the mobile unit while model Jo Portaro passed out free records, Wheeler Agency models representing competitor WHK 1420 AM paraded in front of the van carrying signs such as, "New WHK radio is unfair to other stations because it sounds so good." KYW countered later that morning with their own signs including, "KYW welcomes Cleveland's No. 2 station WHK." Competing with Wilson for drive-time listeners were John Holliday on WHK; Bill Gordon on WJW; Tom Armstrong on WGAR and Phil McLean on WERE. Wes Hopkins took over the KYW microphone at 10 A.M.

(Right) The WIXY 1260 PICKETS, June 21, 1966

Jose Feliciano was appearing at La Cave, 10615 Euclid Ave., Billy Joe Royal was headlining at American A-Go Go, 1614 Euclid, the Arena was preparing for the upcoming Rolling Stones concert on Saturday, June 25th and the first Gen. Sheridan tank was set to roll off the assembly line at the Cleveland Tank Plant, when the photograph at right appeared in The Press on Tuesday, June 21, 1966. The accompanying story offered, "Bosses at strikebound Radio Station WIXY, who believe in making the best of a bad situation, threw up a counter picket line at their Euclid Ave. studios yesterday. Management's pickets probably didn't change anyone's mind in the labor dispute, but it did win a unanimous vote from curbside watchers as the best looking team of demonstrators to hit the streets in a long time. The three pickets were shapely models clad in bathing suits. They carried signs touting the musical merits of the station. A glance at right may give other demonstrators ideas on how to attract more attention in the promotion or derision of causes. WIXY, for management-labor oriented readers, in still on strike." Top tunes on the WIXY 1260 music survey at the time were "Hanky Panky," by the Shondells; "Paperback Writer/Rain," by the Beatles; "Muddy Waters," by Johnny Rivers; "Popsicle," by Jan and Dean (on sale at Recordland Stores for 59¢); "Little Girl," by the Syndicates of Sound; "Along Comes Mary," by The Association; "Strangers in the Night," by Frank Sinatra; "You Don't Have to Say You Love Me," by Dusty Springfield; "Red Rubber Ball," by The Cyrcle and "Younger Girl," by the Critters.

**(Left) WHK RADIO GOOD GUYS,
April 22, 1967**

The Buckingham's "Don't You Care," topped the WHK-AM 1420 music survey followed by The Choir's "It's Cold Outside," on Saturday, April 22, 1967, as WHK hosted a three-day Fashion Freakout at Cleveland Arena that weekend. Highlighting the event were concerts by the Jackie Wilson Review, with Aretha Franklin ("Respect" was No. 13 on the WHK survey), on Saturday, April 22nd; Mitch Ryder (Too Many Fish in the Sea), on Sunday, April 23rd; and the Lovin Spoonful with the Blues Magoos, (Pipe Dream), and the Turtles (She'd Rather Be With Me), on Monday, April 24th. The final two concerts were offered at one ticket price- $3.00. Set for the mod, mod 60's fashion scene of mini skirts, bell bottoms, Twiggy suits, Beatle boots and Monkee shades that weekend were WHK super jocks Len Anthony (left), Rick Shaw, Bob Friend, Mighty Mitch, Ken Scott, Al James and Mort Crowley (right).

**(Right) THE BEACH BOYS,
October 12, 1967**

It was "Fun, Fun, Fun," for thirty WIXY 1260 contest winners who went backstage between shows at Music Hall to meet the Beach Boys with WIXY disc jockeys Larry Morrow (third from left), and Bobby Magic (right), on Thursday, October 12, 1967. Questions ranging from LSD and drugs, to the war in Vietnam, were posed to the California quintet by the inquisitive contest winners. Appearing with the Beach Boys that night were the Box Tops, Ohio Express and Lou (King) Kirby and the U. S. Male. From left to right are Dennis Wilson; Al Jardine; Carl Wilson; Bruce Johnston, the group's newest member; and Mike Love.

(Left) WHK RADIO DOES "GREASE," June 9, 1978

While area movie theaters were featuring such hits as "Saturday Night Fever;" "Star Wars" and "Close Encounters;" "Grease" was the word in Cleveland on Friday, June 9, 1978, when WHK-AM switched its format that weekend from country to "fabulous fifties," celebrating preview showings of the hit film musical "Grease" that evening at Loew's East and the following night at Loew's Yorktown. Joining WHK DJ Paxton Mills on Friday night was "Grease" co-star Stockard Channing, who appeared at both shows. At left are fellow WHK personalities Gary Dee (left), Cynthia Smith, Terry Stevens, Ray Hoffman, J. R. Nelson, Doc Lemon, Carolyn Carr and Jim Crocker (right).

Television
Comes to Cleveland

December 17, 1947

Life in Cleveland changed dramatically on Wednesday, December 17, 1947, when WEWS-TV went on the air as the nation's 11th commercial television station. Station executives chose a live remote from the 13th annual Cleveland Press Christmas Charity Show at Public Hall for the inaugural broadcast. **(Above Right)** Press Show master of ceremonies Jimmy Stewart (left), meets with

Television Time

Scripps Howard Radio president Jack R. Howard (center), and WEWS general manager James C. Hanrahan before the show. While over 8,500 watched local amateurs perform for prizes at Public Hall, television sets across the city were tuned to Channel 5, including five sets in the Higbee Co. auditorium, where TV execs joined an estimated 400 watching the triumphant broadcast. Press radio columnist Stanley Anderson wrote the next day, "I didn't always see The Press Christmas Show emcee clearly, but I saw him well enough to know that he pretended to be disconcerted when he played the accordion." The three men met in front of the station's new mobile broadcast trailer at left.

**WEWS-TV
Dec. 17, 1954**

9:00	Telecourse
9:30	Garry Moore
11:00	Dione Lucas
11:30	Strike It Rich
Noon	Valiant Lady
12:15	Love of Life
12:30	Search for Tomorrow
12:45	Guiding Light
1:00	Women's Window
1:30	Welcome Travelers
2:00	Robert Q. Lewis
2:30	Art Linkletter
3:00	Big Payroll
3:30	Bob Crosby Show
4:00	Mixing Bowl
4:30	Your Account
5:00	Uncle Jake
5:15	Eisenhower
5:30	Twenty Fingers
5:45	Pet; Dinner Platter
6:00	Dinner Platter
6:30	Dorothy Fuldheim
6:45	Sports Page
7:00	Corliss Archer
7:30	Douglas Edwards
7:45	Perry Como
8:00	Mame
8:30	Topper
9:00	Star Playhouse
9:30	Our Miss Brooks
10:00	The Line-Up
10:30	I Led Three Lives
11:00	Playhouse
12:30	News: Sign Off

(Left) CELEBRATING SEVEN YEARS OF BROADCASTING AT WEWS-TV, December 17, 1954

In honor of WEWS-TV's seventh birthday on Wednesday, December 17, 1954, The Press saluted Channel 5's seven senior on-air personalities, Paige Palmer (far left), Crandall Hendershott, Rachel Van Cleve, Bob Dale, Randy Culver, Dorothy Fuldheim and Gene Carroll (lower center).

(Below) Paige Palmer & Ed Allen, October 16, 1961

A special guest on "The Paige Palmer Show" the week of October 16, 1961, was muscle-bound Ed Allen (right, at left). "Allen is the strong man who once attracted a large feminine audience on Channel 8 before he retired," reported The Press. The Paige Palmer Show aired Monday through Friday at 10 A.M. on WEWS-TV, Channel 5. Competing against Palmer on Channel 8 at 10 A.M. was the second hour of Ernie's Place, a movie show hosted by Ernie Anderson.

(Right) WJW-TV'S BANDSTAND SHOW, January 4, 1959

WJW-TV's programming schedule on Saturday, January 4, 1959 included family favorites "Captain Kangaroo;" "Mighty Mouse;" "Heckel & Jeckel;" "Rex Humbard;" "Annie Oakley;" "The Lone Ranger;" "Sea Hunt;" "Perry Mason;" "Gale Storm;" "Have Gun, Will Travel" and "Gunsmoke." Also on the Channel 8 schedule that day was the locally-produced rock-n-roll show "Bandstand," at right, which aired at 1:30

P.M. In November 1959, WJW-Radio DJ Casey Kasem replaced Bandstand host Phil McLean, who started with the show when it aired on WEWS-TV before moving to Channel 8.

Reporting the News at Channel 3

(Right) DICK GODDARD JOINS THE KYW-TV NEWS STAFF, June 28, 1961

On Wednesday, June 28, 1961, Press reporter Carol Weiss wrote, "Northeastern Ohio has many distinctions, but of one it is not proud. That is its top rating as one of the most changeable weather areas in the country. Because of the extreme weather conditions, KYW-TV has hired Dick Goddard, an honest-to-goodness meteorologist, as a weathercaster. Goddard, who does the KYW-TV noon and 6:40 P.M. weather report with such conviction, has already felt a growing interest among youngsters in meteorology. (He has been with the station only since March 1.) He is organizing a network of suburban youngsters to serve as weather observers. With the proper equipment supplied by the station, these amateur meteorologists will report on the snow depths, conditions and rainfall."

(Above right) Dick Goddard (left), with fellow KYW newscasters, Bill Jorgensen, Bud Dancy and Jim Graner (right).

1961

1981

(Right) THE CHANNEL 3 ACTION NEWS TEAM, March, 1981

In March of 1981, the Associated Press named the WKYC-TV Action3News team at right the "outstanding news operation" in the state of Ohio. Left to right are weatherman Al Rokar, Mona Scott, who served as consumer anchor and 11 P.M. co-anchor; Dave Patterson, co-anchor of the 6 P.M. news; Doug Adair, co-anchor at 6 P.M. and 11 P.M.; and sports reporter Joe Pelligrino.

(Above) CAPTAIN PENNY AND MISS BARBARA, February 15, 1960

Former Romper Room headmistress Miss Barbara (Mrs. Barbara Plummer), appeared with Captain Penny (Ron Penfound), as she prepared to bring her teaching techniques to Captain Penny's Noon Show beginning on Monday, February 15, 1960. The Noon Show aired daily on WEWS-TV, Channel 5.

(Upper right) ROBERT WAGNER, August, 1962

During an appearance with Dorothy Fuldheim on the One O'Clock Club in August of 1962, handsome Hollywood heartthrob Robert Wagner hopped behind one of the Channel 5 cameras used on the set.

(Above) AT SANTA'S TOYSHOP, November 19, 1960

WEWS-TV's Christmas special, which aired at 6 P. M. on Friday, November 19, 1960, featured local favorites The Playlady (Pat Dopp) left, and Mr. Jingeling (Max Ellis) in Santa's Toyshop.

(Left) THE KYW-TV CHRISTMAS SHOW, December 22, 1964

"Keep your eye and ear on Weatherman Dick-he's good," offered Press TV-Radio critic Bill Barrett on Monday, December 21, 1964, prior to KYW-TV's holiday special "Three Nights Before Christmas" airing the next night on Channel 3. Featured on the show were local KYW radio and TV personalities Mike Douglas; Jerry G (next to Douglas;) Jay Lawrence (behind G;) John "Bud" Dancy; Jim Runyon (behind Dancy;) Pat Murray; Barnaby (Linn Sheldon;) weatherman Dick Goddard; Jim Axel; Carl Stern and Woodrow the Woodsman (Clay Conroy.) Also pictured is Dorothy Collins of Hit Parade fame. The show aired at 7:30 P.M. opposite "Combat" on Channel 5 and "The Defenders" on Channel 8. Following the Channel 3 special at 8:30 P.M. was "The Man from U.N.C.L.E."

The Mike Douglas Show

(Right) Merv Griffin and the British rock group, "Freddie and Dreamers," joined co-host Carol Lawrence (at the piano), on "The Mike Douglas Show," when the photograph at right was taken for a story in The Press on Friday, April 23, 1965. The show, which aired daily at 12:30 P.M. on KYW-TV, was produced locally at the Channel 3 studios.

(Left) WITH NANCY AMES, January 14, 1965

"That Was The Week That Was" girl Nancy Ames (with Douglas at left), joined Errol Garner and Eugene Methvin, author of "How Reds Make a Riot," on the Thursday, January 14, 1965 edition of "The Mike Douglas Show."

(Right) WITH BILL COSBY

On the Monday, January 25, 1965 edition of "The Mike Douglas Show," comedian Bill Cosby joined guest host George Goebel, Celeste Holm, Chad and Jeremy and singer Susan Barrett. At right, Cosby hams it up on an earlier show with Douglas and Marie Walther, a member of the 1964 Olympic gymnastic squad.

(Right, Below) Some Queen for a Day hopefuls (right and below), left home before 7 A.M. to be first in line on Friday, January 30, 1948, for the 2 P.M. broadcast of "Queen for a Day" over WHK Radio. The lobby doors at Public Hall weren't scheduled to be opened until 12:30 P.M., but with hundreds of determined, but freezing, women waiting outside the hall, management opened the Lakeside Avenue doors a half hour early. **(Inset)** Miss Maria SantaMaria pours coffee for Mrs. Jennie Venturo, who told a reporter, "I came early just to see Jack Bailey."

Queen For A Day

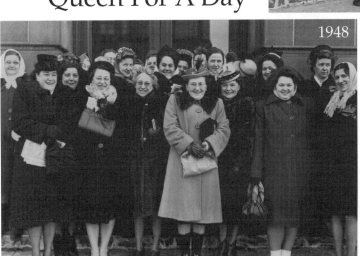

1948

1963

(Left) Emcee Jack Bailey poses with 28-year-old mother of seven, Mrs. William Ciccarello of Auburndale Ave., who was crowned Queen For a Day by Bailey during his ABC-TV show at Music Hall on Tuesday, May 7, 1963. Among the prizes she received were 2,000 Eagle Stamps, a dinette set, a sewing machine, a clothes dryer, a $1,000 shopping spree from the Spiegel catalog, and $200 Pick-n-Pay grocery certificates. The show aired daily at 3 P.M. on Channel 5.

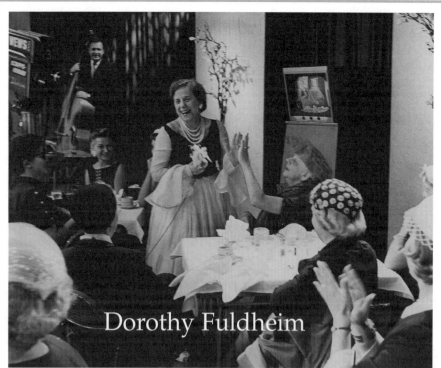

Dorothy Fuldheim

(Left) As WEWS-TV prepared to celebrate its 10th anniversary on Monday, December 16, 1957, one of the more popular live programs airing locally was the "One O'Clock Club" hosted by Dorothy Fuldheim (center), who began working at Channel 5 before the station hit the airwaves on December 17, 1947. By 1959, the "One O'Clock Club" was the only major daily TV show produced locally.

(Lower left) Dorothy takes a break with co-host Bill "Smoochie" Gordon on the set of the "One O' Clock Club," as the show entered its sixth year on Monday, August 27, 1962. The show aired daily at 1 P.M. on Channel 5. Seven Keys followed at 2 P.M.

(Below) Dorothy appears on the "One O'Clock Club" set with Cleveland-native Bob Hope, who was taping a week-long series of shows with Fuldheim that began on Monday, May 20, 1963. Among the topics discussed was Hope's new book, "I Owe Russia $1200," which was being serialized in The Press. Competing for audience share with the 90-minute One O'Clock Club on Channel 5, was "The Mike Douglas Show," on Channel 3; and "Password," on Channel 8.

WITH BARBARA WALTERS,
February 8, 1982

Fuldheim, the dean of Cleveland broadcasters, questions ABC-TV newswoman Barbara Walters (right), for a television interview that aired over WEWS-TV on Monday, February 8, 1982. Mrs. Fuldheim was the only local journalist to interview Miss Walters, who was in town to speak before more than 2,000 at Stouffer's Inn on the Square.

(Right) Before joining WJW-TV, Ernie Anderson spent time at WHK Radio as an on-air personality. At right, Anderson receives a kiss from lovely Kay Crobaugh after winning a celebrity motor boat race, one of six races sponsored by the Marine Trades Association at the Forest City Yacht Club on Sunday, July 14, 1958. **(Below)** Connie Gill, winner of a Teen-age Summer Job Contest, receives a quickie course in radio work from Anderson and fellow WHK disc jockey Tom Brown (left), at the WHK studios in July of 1958.

(Below right)
August 11, 1961

When the photograph below right appeared in The Press on Friday, August 11, 1961, the caption read, "Fit to be necktied in a tight go-kart race is Ernie Anderson (left), WJW-TV movie host and Tom (Tim) Conway, comedian, writer and director of Ernie's Place seen Monday through Friday at 9:30 on Channel 8." Conway and Anderson were long-time friends.

(Far right) April 28, 1963

Anderson posed with area teens for a story in The Press about his Ghoulardi character on Friday, April 28, 1963. In addition to hosting WJW's late night show on Friday nights, Anderson had just begun hosting a Saturday show at 6 P.M. on Channel 8.

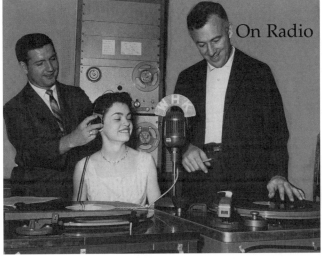

On Radio

Ernie Anderson a.k.a. Ghoulardi

On Television

GHOULARDI'S ALL-STARS
April 29, 1966

As "Ghoulardi's All-Stars" prepared to play Channel 5 in their first softball game of the season on Friday, April 29, 1966, (proceeds went to new Rainbow Babies and Childrens Hospital), Press columnist Bill Barrett quoted Anderson (below), as saying, "Big Chuck Schodowski (top left at right),- that's hand-some debonair Jerry Kriegel of Parma Place- is an all-round threat," while "Franz the Toymaker (top row, fourth from left), is our pitcher because he just isn't a very good player."

Liberace Comes to Town, 1954

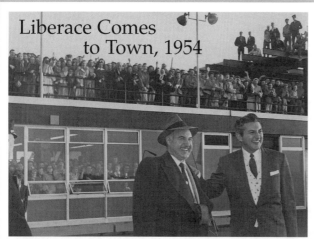

More than 2,000 vocal fans waited in the doorways, behind windows and on the airport's new viewing deck for a glimpse of popular entertainer Wladziv Liberace and his brother George at Cleveland Airport on Thursday, May 20, 1954. Press columnist Stan Anderson wrote the next day, "Liberace's appearance at the airport last night caused confusion because no one since Frank Sinatra has come into town and stirred the populace as this performer did yesterday. They were as vocal and as intense as Sinatra's followers were at the height of the crooner's career." **(Below right)** WERE Radio disc jockey Bill Randle interviewes the flamboyant pianist upon his arrival. Liberace performed that night at Music Hall, changing outfits from an all-white formal to black regulation tails and a smoking jacket.

The Polka King- Frankie Yankovic

(Left) POLKA VARIETIES CELEBRATES ITS 10TH ANNIVERSARY, September 4, 1966

Celebrating the 10th anniversary of WEWS-TV's "Polka Varieties," on Sunday, September 4, 1966, were (left to right), show host Paul Wilcox, producer Herman Spero, program director Al Herrick and polka king Frankie Yankovic, who appeared on the first show in 1956. The hour-long locally produced broadcast aired at 1 P.M. Sundays on Channel 5 following "The Gene Carroll Show."

On December 6, 1941, a young accordionist named Frankie Yankovic, who grew up in Cleveland's Collinwood area, realized a dream by opening a modest cafe at 523 East 152nd St. in the heart of Cleveland's polka land. Less than a decade later, with gold records for "Just Because" and "Blue Skirt Waltz," the talented entertainer won the title of "America's Polka King."

(Right) FRANKIE WITH GEORGE LIBERACE, April 12, 1959

"Polish pals from their leaner days, Frankie Yankovic (seated) and George Liberace are reunited on Frankie's polka cast Sunday," offered The Press on Saturday, April 11, 1959. Appearing with Liberace on the hour-long polka party the next day were Linda Yankovic and Eddie Habat. In addition to "The Frankie Yankovic Show" at 1 P.M., the April 12th schedule on Channel 5 included the "Gene Carroll Show" at noon; the Cleveland Indians-Kansas City Royals baseball game; "The Lone Ranger;" "Jim Bowie;" "Roy Rogers;" "Lassie;" "Maverick;" "Law Man;" "Colt .45;" "I Am the Law;" "D. A.'s Man;" and "Meet McGraw" at 10:30 P.M.

1965

Cleveland
Welcomes

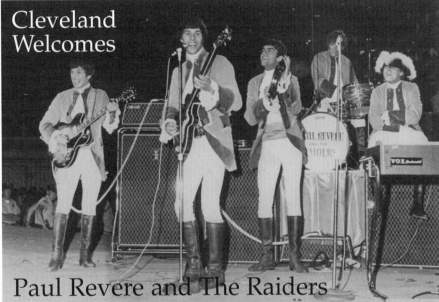

Paul Revere and The Raiders

1966

(Upper right) WHK Radio's Joe Mayer (center,) rides with Paul Revere and the Raiders to promote WHK Appreciation Day at Geauga Lake Park on Tuesday, August 24, 1965. Also appearing were Sonny and Cher and the Shangrillas.

(Above, Right) Paul Revere and the Raiders headlined the Press Spirit of '66 Fun 'n Fashions Festival at Public Hall on Wednesday, August 24, 1966. Tickets ranged from $1.50 to $3.50 for the 8,000 who saw The Raiders along with Chad and Jeremy, Tommy Roe, Jeff Kutash and the Upbeat dancers, and five local bands- Muther's Oats, Trohls, Mixed Emotions, Tree Stumps and the Saxons. Upbeat host Don Webster, Ken Scott of WHK and WIXY's Jack Armstrong served as emcees. **(Above)** Lead singer Mark Lindsay. **(Above right)** Jim Valley (left), Phil Volk, Lindsay, Mike Smith and Paul Revere.

1967

(Left, Above) Paul Revere and Mark Lindsay, the two original Raiders, met fans before a WIXY 1260-sponsored concert on Sunday, April 9, 1967. The Cleveland Arena crowd of over 4,000 (above), rocked to the group's top 10 hits including "Hungry," "Ups and Downs," "Just Like Me," "Good Thing" and "Kicks." Lindsay told the crowd, "Cleveland is one of our favorite places to play. Thanks for everything, we love you."

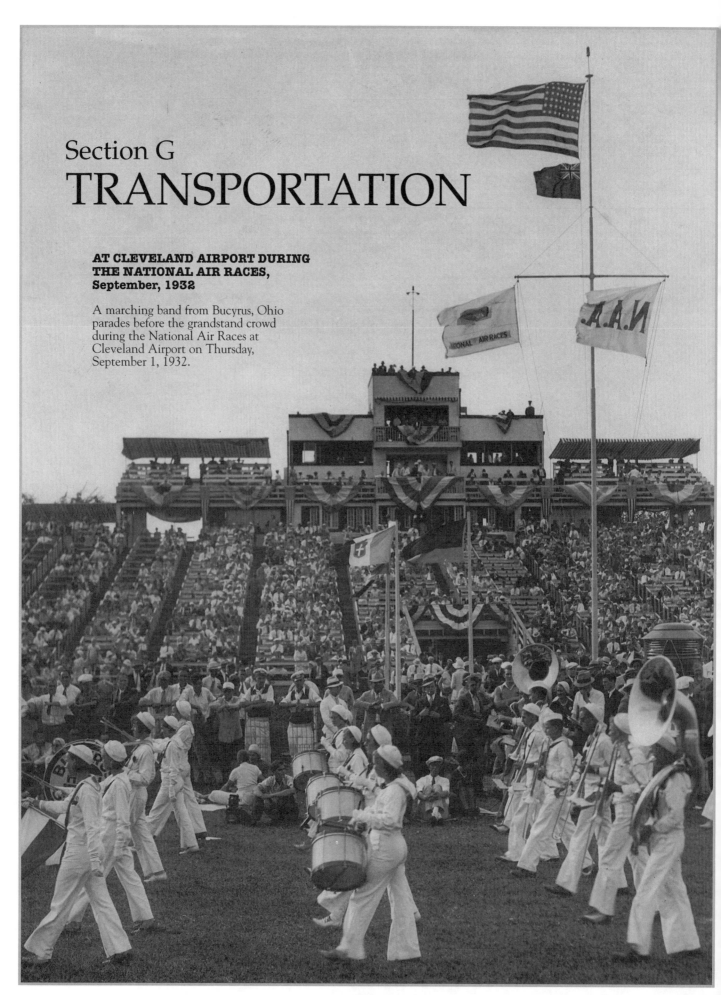

Section G
TRANSPORTATION

AT CLEVELAND AIRPORT DURING THE NATIONAL AIR RACES, September, 1932

A marching band from Bucyrus, Ohio parades before the grandstand crowd during the National Air Races at Cleveland Airport on Thursday, September 1, 1932.

(Above) STREETCAR OVERCROWDING, October 19, 1921

After Concon officials announced a further reduction in streetcar service during the winter months, The Press reported on Friday, October 19, 1921, "About 60 percent of the riders were women. They received little consideration whether in getting to the entrance or getting seats. So few are the cars that each one looks out for himself." The most serious nightly bottleneck was stated to be at the southwest corner of W. Superior and Public Square (above), where, "at times there were more than 500 would-be passengers massed at the corner," waiting for cars headed for stops on Denison Avenue, Detroit Avenue and Clifton Boulevard.

**(Left)
NEEDING NEW
STREETCARS,
September 3, 1940**

"City officials and executives of the Cleveland Railway Co. differ on many policies, but both agree that the system, and especially the riding equipment, must be modernized," The Press reported on Thursday, September 3, 1940. While the railway company had already begun purchasing new busses to replace antiquated streetcars, a number of streetcars dating back to 1913, 1914 and 1915 were still running on the Cedar, Scovill, Detroit and Clifton lines. The newspaper compared the streetcar at left, built in 1923, to another means of transportation built that year, a 1923 Rickenbacker automobile. The most modern street cars running at the time were purchased in 1929.

(Left)
AT THE NATIONAL AIR RACES

More than 100 planes took part in the Opening Day program when the National Air Races, held for the third time in Cleveland, opened at Cleveland Airport on Saturday, August 27, 1932. The 10-day air carnival began at 1 P.M. with a series of aerial demonstrations, while planes participating in the Cord Cup transcontinental race began arriving from Cincinnati. At left, Army Air Corps planes reach the main runway on Sunday, August 28th, when over 25,000 attended the weekend program. Attendance figures ranged from 178,000 to 300,000, including free passes, generating an estimated $267,000 from $1 general admission tickets, grandstand seats ranging from $1.50 to $5 and $300 event boxes.

The 1932 National Air Races At Cleveland Airport

(Below) JAMES H. HAIZLIP WINS THE BENDIX TROPHY, August 31st

On Wednesday, August 31, 1932, St. Louis pilot James H. Haizlip established a new Los Angeles to New York speed record by reaching New York in 10 hours, 19 minutes, breaking Maj. James H. Doolittle's transcontinental record of 11 hours, 16 minutes by nearly an hour. After his record-breaking trip, Haizlip (leaving his Wendell-Williams racer below), flew to Cleveland where he was handed the Bendix Trophy as some 20,000 race show spectators looked on. Haizlip won the trophy by being the first pilot to reach Cleveland from Los Angeles. After flashing over Cleveland to claim the Bendix race and its $6,750 grand prize, Haizlip, averaging 245 m.p.h., streaked on to New York where he won an additional $2,500 for breaking the transcontinental record.

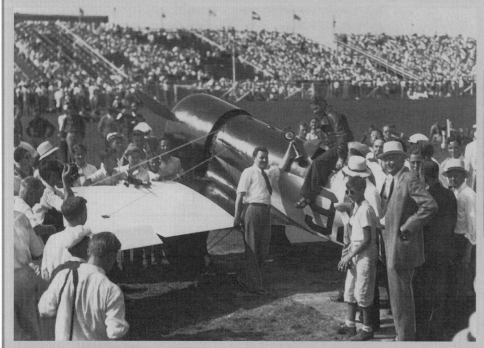

(Above) DOOLITTLE WINS THE THOMPSON TROPHY RACE

Famed aviator Jimmy Doolittle walks to the public address system after winning the 100-mile Thompson Trophy race during the National Air Races on Monday, September 5, 1932.

(Above) September 1st Parachutist Robert Ray hits the 100-foot bullseye at Cleveland Airport during the National Air Races on Thursday, September 1, 1932.

(Above) AMELIA EARHART AT THE NATIONAL AIR RACES, September 2nd

Aviatrix Amelia Earhart Putnam (above far right), relaxes during the Air Races on Friday, September 2, 1932, with Frances Marsalis (left), Peggy Lennox, Blanche Noyes, Peggy Raney, Jean La Rene and Loretta Schumacher (right). On September 1st, Earhart was among fourteen lady flyers meeting at Hotel Westlake where a request was drafted to have races designated for women only. The pilots hoped to participate in a female-only transcontinental derby and a separate series of closed circuit races for lady racers. The proposed women's derby was designed to run from Portland, Oregon to Cleveland, in a two-race format- one race for planes reaching speeds up to 125 m.p.h. and another for planes over 125 m.p.h. Earhart sponsored the Amelia Earhart Trophy race on the 2nd, won by Florence Klingensmith, who took home the George Palmer Putnam cup and a new automobile. During the presentation ceremony, the participants had to quickly dash for cover when a policeman alertly pointed to a group of parachutists bearing down directly above them.

PUSHER PLANE MEETS AUTOGYRO, Sept. 3rd

During a low altitude mock battle between a vintage 1910 "pusher" plane and an autogyro on Saturday, September 3, 1932, the pusher plane (top), collided with the autogyro (above), piloted by Johnny Miller, as the two prepared to land. While Miller and a Press reporter, who was riding as a passenger, walked away unhurt, veteran motion picture stuntman Al Wilson, the pusher plane pilot, died the next day at Berea Community Hospital after being pinned under the wreckage. Wilson's death was the first directly related to the Air Show.

(Right) WATCHING THE RACES, August 30th

Protected from the sun by their Japanese parasols, Miss Mary Gallagher (left), Mrs. Neil Devine and Miss Mercedes Hurley take in The National Air Races on Tuesday, August 30, 1932.

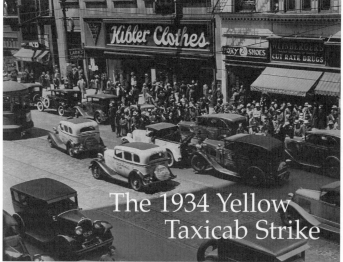

The 1934 Yellow
Taxicab Strike

After "an uproarious before-dawn meeting," drivers from Taxicab Drivers' Union No. 555 voted to strike for union recognition and a "living wage," on Thursday, May 3, 1934, grounding 497 taxis of the Yellow Cab Company. On Saturday, May 26th, downtown Cleveland served as the battleground between union sympathizers and Yellow Cab drivers when the company attempted to provide service with drivers who had formed their own organization. On Sunday, May 27th, four Yellow Cabs returned to the garage unharmed after touring the city under police escort. But on Monday, May 28th, the violence escalated when eleven cabs, with heavy screening covering their windows, paraded down Euclid Avenue at noontime under police protection. When the convoy reached Playhouse Square near E. 13th St., a score of men began hurling pieces of brick, concrete and iron pipe at the vehicles, continuing the assault until the cabs passed Public Square. At the time, Yellow Cab was paying a minimum wage of $12 a week, with no fines or deductions, but had also agreed to pay for all gasoline used, provide drivers 35 per cent of all bookings in excess of the minimum wage and fix the work week at 54 hours.

(Above left) On Saturday, May 26th, downtown Cleveland became the scene of bloody attacks when the Yellow Cab Co.

sent out thirty cars driven by non-union drivers in an effort to break the 23-day strike. As the taxis became separat-

ed by mobs of attackers, drivers began deserting their cars along Euclid Avenue. In front of Kibler's Clothes, a driver was slugged and dragged out of his taxi. Windows in his cab were shattered, ignition wires ripped out and the tires deflated. The attackers also tried to tip his car over but failed. **(Above)** Spectators gather outside Mills Restaurant on Euclid Avenue where damaged Yellow taxis blocked traffic.

(Top) After forcing a driver to flee his taxi at Public Square on the 26th, the victim's attackers hopped on the running board of their getaway car as a policeman helped the shaken driver.

(Above) A Yellow Cab driver is led to safety on the 26th after being dragged from his car, beaten and knocked to the ground. Another driver had his nose broken, three teeth knocked out and his faced bloodied by flying glass.

(Left) Yellow Cab taxis jam the intersection of E. Ninth and Euclid on Monday, May 28, 1934 under the barrage of bricks thrown by attackers.

(Right) JOHNNY KILBANE RETURNS, March 17, 1912

"Cleveland went Kilbane-mad Sunday afternoon," reported The Press on March 18, 1912, after boxer Johnny Kilbane returned home on March 17th as the city's first world title holder. Kilbane beat Abe Atell in California to capture the feather-weight boxing title. After departing Union Depot, the little Irishman, seated in the car at right with his wife and their baby Coletta, was welcomed back by over 100,000 raucous St. Patrick's Day faithful as the boxer's car caravan traveled along downtown streets. Standing bareheaded in the auto as he saluted his fans, Kilbane proudly carried his daughter under one arm and an American flag in his other hand.

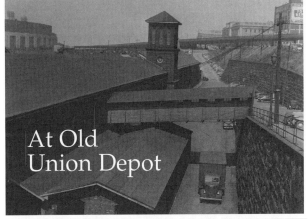

At Old Union Depot

(Left, Below) UNION DEPOT, March 26, 1946

Press reporter Robert Bordner described Pennsylvania Railroad's once proud 81-year-old Union Depot near Municipal Stadium as, "grimy with soot, rotting in dingy senility, without a taxi stand, without even street-car service," on Tuesday, March 26, 1946, while his paper called the station, "Cleveland's No. 1 Eyesore." Bordner wrote, "Now Clevelanders come home from Bataan and Iwo Jima, from El Alamein and Aachen and Berlin, some of them to the same old station their great-grandfathers used some 70 years ago." Only one redcap remained on duty.

(Left) THE CY YOUNG DAY PARADE, June 11, 1947

It was "Cy Young Day" at Municipal Stadium on Wednesday, June 11, 1947, as the legendary 80-year-old Hall of Fame pitcher was honored before the Cleveland Indians game with the Boston Red Sox. When the former Cleveland Naps great arrived by train with "the entire town" of Newcomerstown, OH, his hometown, Tribe owner Bill Veeck welcomed the expected group of 5,000 with a parade from Union Depot to the Stadium. **(Left)** A marching band leads the way as the guests of honor head to Municipal Stadium. At the Stadium, Young received a number of gifts and was joined by several former teammates including Tris Speaker, Jack Graney, Elmer Flick, Bill Bradley, Glen Liebhardt, Paddy Livingstone and Jack Delahanty. Young later told The Press that modern pitchers have a harder time of it than the ancients did. "Shucks, we used that old blacked up ball," Young recalled. "Nobody paid any attention to it. Why, we would have painted a stripe on it." When asked whom he considered to be the fastest pitcher in history, Cy replied, "Stand up Walter Johnson, Bob Feller and Cy Young in a line and the answer would be... no difference."

Section H
POLITICS

(OPPOSITE PAGE) February 18, 1958

Here to address the first Cleveland Press Book and Author Luncheon of the season in Hotel Carter's Rainbow Room on Thursday, February 18, 1958, Senator John Fitzgerald Kennedy was greeted by Press Editor Louis B. Seltzer and mayor Anthony J. Celebreeze (right), upon arriving at Cleveland Airport. Kennedy was invited to speak following the release of his Pulitzer-prize winning book "Profiles in Courage" (Harper, $3.00).

(Right) AS SENATOR, September 21, 1958

Describing it as the largest political gathering he had ever seen, 41-year-old Massachusetts senator John F. Kennedy spoke before a crowd of well over 65,000 at Euclid Beach Park during the annual Democratic steer roast on Sunday, September 21, 1958. **(Right)** Kennedy and wife Jackie are greeted by well-wishers as they walked through the park.

Kennedy Visits

(Right) AS CANDIDATE, September 27, 1960

With Senator Frank J. Lausche at his side, Democratic candidate Senator John F. Kennedy hit the campaign trail throughout Northern Ohio on Tuesday, September 27, 1960. Kennedy was making his second appearance in Cleveland in three days. After addressing attendees at Euclid Beach Park during the annual Democratic Steer Roast on Sunday, September 25th, Kennedy flew to Chicago for his first televised debate with Republican candidate Richard M. Nixon on Monday, September 26th. Immediately following the debate, Kennedy flew back to Painesville where he spent the night. On the 27th, Kennedy embarked on the car caravan at right that took the charismatic politician through Public Square to Lakewood, Rocky River, Lorain and Mansfield. Kennedy then flew by plane to Akron and Canton. **(Right)** As the motorcade reached downtown Cleveland, police were caught short-handed when thousands rushed the vehicles traveling along Euclid Avenue.

(Right) AS PRESIDENT, October 19, 1962

It was a beautiful fall day on Friday, October 19, 1962, when the President of the United States, John F. Kennedy, on the campaign trail securing voter support for the Democratic ticket, came to town for an appearance at Public Square. After leaving Cleveland Hopkins Airport, Kennedy's motorcade stopped along the way to let area residents meet the nation's chief executive. He first greeted youngsters at Our Lady of Mount Carmel School at W. 70th and Detroit Ave., and then stopped to greet students and teachers at St. Edward High School, where he was given a football while the St. Edward High band played in the background. **(Right)** Kennedy is mobbed by well-wishers as he approached the massive crowd on the Square. With Kennedy were Senator Frank J. Lausche and Governor Michael DiSalle (right).

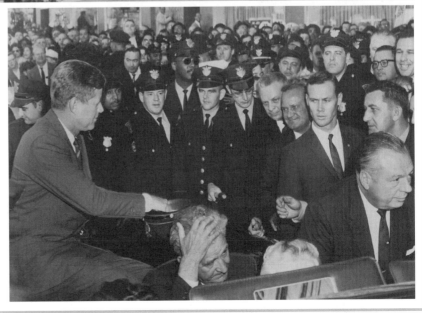

President Hoover Arrives

October 2, 1930

"President Hoover is in town," proclaimed The Press on Thursday, October 2, 1930, after a special train with the nation's 31st president aboard arrived at 11:50 A.M. from Philadelphia. Troops A and B of the 107th Cavalry, O. N. G. (above), led the way, as the chief executive's entourage headed from Pennsylvania Railroad's E. 55th St.-Euclid Avenue depot to Public Square. Hoover was scheduled to appear at a series of receptions and concerts before delivering the keynote address at the American Banker's Association convention that evening in Public Hall. The Press reported, "Temper of the crowd varied as the parade moved along. At E. 18th Street, where spectators were jammed in triple and quadruple rows, they cheered. At E. Ninth Street they clapped hands and whistled shrilly. Although the crowd was an enormous one, it was not an unusually demonstrative one. Men outnumbered women along the whole line. After the greeting and cheers and applause, a silence fell until the parading autos had passed into the next central point. Trooping into the street behind the parade, the spectators (above right), prevented any immediate resumption of traffic."

(Right) Hoover heads down Euclid Avenue with his wife.

Our Nation's Leaders Come to Cleveland

GENERAL DWIGHT D. EISENHOWER,

April 11, 1946

Less than eight months after the end of World War II, General of the Army, Dwight D. Eisenhower, arrived at Cleveland Airport on Thursday, April 11, 1946, to speak before members of the Cleveland Aviation Club. Before reaching Public Square, Eisenhower's 21-car caravan stopped at the NACA laboratory at Cleveland Airport and briefly at Lakewood High, where General Eisenhower was given the school's coat of arms. As confetti and ticker tape rained from above, one of largest turnouts in local memory greeted the general as he motored along Euclid Avenue at left. That evening, he spoke to 1,600 guests in Hotel Carter's Rainbow Room.

PRESIDENT HARRY S. TRUMAN, October 9, 1952

Public Square was jammed with spectators as President Harry S. Truman came to town with his daughter Margaret (third from left at right), on Thursday, October 9, 1952. The retiring chief executive, who was on a 24-state "whistle-stop" train tour stumping for Democratic candidates, was invited here by County Democratic Chairman Ray T. Miller.

(Above) Ray T. Miller speaks to the crowd before Truman's arrival at Union Terminal.

(Right) Truman delivers his 20-minute speech from the platform in front of Terminal Tower.

(Right) CANDIDATE RICHARD M. NIXON, October 6, 1960

"With this demonstration we can carry Cuyahoga County for Richard Nixon," proclaimed Cuyahoga County Republican chairman A. L. (Sonny) De Maioribus, following the rousing local reception Republican candidate Richard M. Nixon received on Thursday, October 6, 1960. After arriving at Burke Lakefront Airport a half hour late, Nixon's motorcade was further delayed by the crowds that surged his car. At right, Nixon and his wife address the crowd at E. Ninth and Euclid, one of several times the presidential candidate spoke to the estimated crowd of 125,000. Veteran policemen said the jam that halted Nixon's convertible at E. Ninth and Euclid was the largest ever seen there. After arriving at Hotel Cleveland, Nixon ate dinner, rested briefly, and then headed to Public Hall where he addressed a standing room only crowd of 18,000 supporters. Later that night, Nixon flew to Washington for the second televised Kennedy-Nixon presidential debate.

(Left) PRESIDENT LYNDON B. JOHNSON COMES TO TOWN, June 17, 1964

Mayor Ralph S. Locher urged everyone to give the President, "a real old fashioned Cleveland welcome," as the nation's chief executive came here to speak during the Communication Workers convention at Public Hall on Wednesday, June 17, 1964. When crowds blocked the north-south roadways through the Square, LBJ stopped his motorcade and began mingling with spectators. Johnson walked from one side of Superior Ave. to the other, shaking hands with the throngs of onlookers as secret service agents anxiously circled the man from Texas. Johnson returned to his vehicle, but as he neared E. Sixth St., he left the car again to greet supporters.

(Above) Delegates pack Public Hall during one of the sessions. **(Above)** Former President Herbert Hoover (above left), prepares to address the convention and a national radio audience on June 10th. Among the California delegates was producer-director Cecil B. DeMille. **(Left)** As the convention opened on Tuesday, June 9th, a covered wagon drawn by four oxen was parked on the east side of Public Hall. **(Below)** Conventioneers flood the street in front of Auditorium Hotel at the corner of E. 6th and St. Clair.

"Within the historic walls of Public Hall, where Calvin Coolidge was nominated for the presidency 12 years ago, the twenty-first national gathering of the Republican Party met today to name its champion against the New Deal," wrote Press Politics Editor Richard L. Maher on Tuesday, June 9, 1936, after the Republican National Convention opened in Cleveland. On Thursday, June 11th, 16,000 conventioneers rocked the hall with celebratory cheers after nominating Kansas Gov. Albert (Alf) Mossman Landon to face President Franklin D. Roosevelt in the November election.

June 9 - 11, 1936

Cleveland Hosts the Republican National Convention

(Above) An auto from Maryland attracted attention on Euclid Avenue. **(Above right)** With City Hall in the background, musicians supporting Gov. Alf Landon marched along E. 6th before the Republican convention opened on June 9th.

(Below) **HERBERT HOOVER ARRIVES, June 10th**

(Below left) Mayor Harold H. Burton, Charles P. Fletcher, chairman of the Republican National Committee and Police Chief George J. Matowitz (all to Hoover's left), were among the dignitaries greeting Hoover (center), upon his arrival at Union Terminal on Wednesday, June 10th. **(Below)** Hoover, the only living former president at the time, makes his way to the podium in Public Hall on the 10th.

PEGGY ANN LANDON ARRIVES, June 9, 1936

Adding a homey touch to the convention on Tuesday, June 9, 1936, was the arrival of Gov. Alf Landon's daughter, 19-year-old University of Kansas sophomore Peggy Ann Landon and father, 79-year-old John M. Landon.

(Right) Miss Landon responds to questions from several dozen reporters "with the skill of a fencer."

(Far right) Peggy Ann pins a Landon ribbon on her grandfather before her father received the G.O.P. nomination on June 11th.

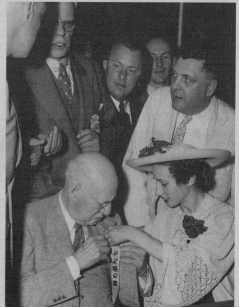

City Politics

(Left) HUEY LONG COMES TO TOWN, April 23, 1932

Press reporter Julian Griffin described Senator Huey P. Long (far left), as "the petrel of southern politics," on Saturday, April 23, 1932, after the stocky politician arrived here to speak before the City Club on "What is Wrong With Us." With Long is Senator Robert Bulkley (second from left), and Cleveland Indians owner Alva Bradley (right). Long had become a minority stockholder in the Indians while serving as Governor of Louisiana. At the time, the Indians held their spring training camp in New Orleans.

(Middle left) MAYORS BURTON AND LA GUARDIA, October 29, 1938

"A little man with expressive hands, explosive language and a habit of getting things done in a big way," is how Press reporter William Townes described mayor of New York Fiorello La Guardia on Saturday, October 29, 1938. La Guardia (right, at left), was in town to speak for the civil service extension amendment that evening at Masonic Auditorium. "The size of Cleveland is ideal," La Guardia told his friend mayor Harold H. Burton (far left), when the two met at Hotel Cleveland that morning. "When you get beyond a million population, costs increase greater than the population," the visiting mayor explained. Burton agreed saying, "That's why I've kept away from moving to New York."

(Below) DAVY CROCKETT COMES TO TOWN, June 15, 1955

Here to promote the opening of Walt Disney's new wide screen technicolor movie "Davy Crockett," on Thursday, June 16, 1955 at the "healthfully air conditioned" RKO Palace Theater, Fess Parker (second from left below), who starred as "Davy Crockett," and Buddy Ebsen (lower right below), who played Crockett's sidekick "George Russel," made a special appearance during Citizen Night at Public Hall on June 15th. During their appearance, requests came in for the men to sing "The Ballad of Davy Crockett," the new movie's popular theme song. Discovering that the Crockett guitar had been left behind, the men shook the hands of some 2,000 youngsters on hand to see "The King of the Wild Frontier."

(Left) Parker, who said, "let the kids come up and we'll shake their paws," greets his young fans.

(Below) Parker brought out 'Ol' Betsy,' Davy Crockett's muzzle-loading long rifle, to share with Mayor Anthony J. Celebreeze (left), and Governor Frank J. Lausche (center).

MAYOR BURKE & BOB HOPE, 1953

Cleveland native Bob Hope shakes the hand of mayor Thomas A. Burke during an "Assembly of Famous Ohio Personalities" luncheon at Hotel Carter celebrating Ohio's sesquicentennial on Monday, October 19, 1953. Famous Ohioans attending the affair included Johnny Kilbane, Branch Rickey, Milton Caniff, Don Miller and Earl Wilson.

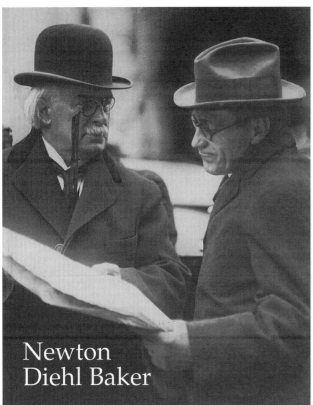

Newton Diehl Baker

(Left) WITH DAVID LLOYD GEORGE, October 23, 1923

On Tuesday, October 23, 1923, former British prime minister David Lloyd George (far left), arrived in Cleveland by train with his wife and daughter. One of his first duties after arriving was participating in the cornerstone laying ceremony for the city's new library building at Superior Avenue and E. Third streets. Over 75,000 crowded along Superior to hear the dedication address from the statesman some writers called the greatest man in the world. Special Ohio Bell amplifiers and loudspeakers were placed on buildings along the street for the crowd to hear the diminutive Welchman. Former U. S. Secretary of War Newton D. Baker (right, at left), joined Lloyd George in addressing the massive gathering.

(Left) Baker and his wife were among the 80,000 watching the Cleveland Indians battle the Philadelphia Athletics in the first pro baseball game played at Municipal Stadium on Sunday, July 31, 1931. The Athletics won, 1-0, as Philadelphia's Lefty Grove beat Tribe starter Mel Harder for the win.

From 10 A.M. to noon on Tuesday, December 28, 1937, more than 3,000 men and women "of every walk of life," including William G. Mather (below center left), and city manager William R. Hopkins (below center right), paid their last respects to former mayor of Cleveland and secretary of war Newton D. Baker, one of the city's most influential lawyers and leading civic citizens. While his body laid at rest in Trinity Episcopal Cathedral at E. 22nd and Euclid Ave. (right), a four-man military guard from Fort Hayes in Columbus stood at the bier. Following a public service at 3 P.M., a private service was held at Lakeview Cemetery where Baker was buried with friends and clients including John D. Rockefeller and James A. Garfield. Among the pallbearers were James C. Hostetler, Thomas L. Sidlo, Paul Patterson and Arthur C. Denison. Hundreds sent their condolences including Secretary of State Cordell Hull, Mrs. Woodrow Wilson, Gen. John J. Pershing, RCA president David Sarnoff, author Walter Lippman, former governor George White and Ohio State University president George W. Rightmire.

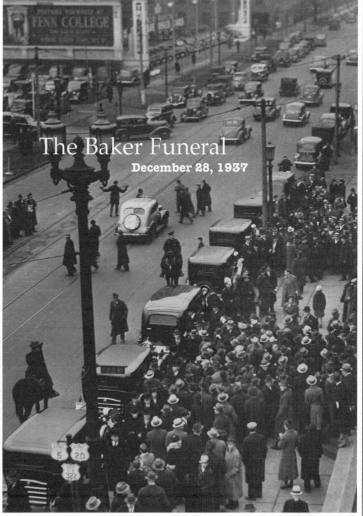

The Baker Funeral
December 28, 1937

(Right)
THE ANNUAL LABOR DAY STEER ROAST,
September 6, 1964

Over 90,000 made it to Euclid Beach Park on Sunday, September 6, 1964 for the Cleveland AFL-CIO Federation of Labor's annual Labor Day picnic and Steer Roast. The principle speaker that day was Welfare Secretary and former Cleveland mayor Anthony J. Celebreeze (at podium), who addressed an enthusiastic crowd of about 1,000 supporters. Celebreeze praised President Lyndon Johnson and the late John F. Kennedy while attacking Johnson's Republican challenger, Barry Goldwater. During his speech, Celebreeze pointed out, "Within the past week, we have just entered our 43rd month of continued economic growth- the longest and strongest peacetime economic expansion in American history."

Carl B. Stokes

(Left) BEING SWORN IN,
November 13, 1967

Elected by just 1,644 votes over Republican challenger Seth C. Taft, 40-year-old attorney and state representative Carl B. Stokes (right), was sworn in as the 50th mayor of Cleveland on Monday, November 13, 1967. When the oath was administered by Judge Anthony A. Rutkowski (far left), Stokes became the first black to serve as mayor of a major American city. With Stokes at the historic ceremony were his brother Louis, his wife Shirley and their children Carl Jr., 8, and Cordi, 6. Over 1,000 supporters attended the inauguration.

(Far left) WITH CYRUS EATON,
December 7, 1967

On Thursday, December 7, 1967, Chesapeake and Ohio Board Chairman Cyrus Eaton (far left), stopped by City Hall to praise the new mayor. Eaton told The Press, "I came in and told Mayor Stokes he has a brilliant beginning, that I wish him good luck." The 83-year-old financier added, "He has undertaken a stupendous job and he has the qualities needed for it."

(Left) WITH BOXER GEORGE
FOREMAN, April 27, 1970

Heavyweight boxer and Olympic Gold Medal winner George Foreman, in town on Monday, April 27, 1970 for a boxing match at the Arena, received the key to the city from Mayor Stokes at City Hall as both men donned boxing gloves. Foreman later traveled to the Salvation Army's Hough Multi-Purpose Center at 6000 Hough Ave., where he participated in an awards ceremony with Olympic gold medalist Madeline Manning Jackson, a staff member at the center.

Tony's Diner

Tony's Diner, the West Side eatery on W. 117th St. where Cleveland Mayor Dennis Kucinich (center), ate breakfast every morning, became the set for a segment for NBC's Tomorrow Show taped with the mayor on Monday, August 14, 1978. Questioning Kucinich, who was in midst of a recall petition, were Tomorrow Show host Tom Snyder (left), television commentator Dorothy Fuldheim, Press Associate Editor Herb Kamm (right), and Plain Dealer Publisher Tom Vail (with back to camera). The segment was set to air at 1 A.M. the following morning.

THE PEACE BREAKFAST
August 24, 1978

Only days after Mayor Dennis Kucinich survived the first recall election in Cleveland history, a "peace breakfast" took place at Tony's Diner on Thursday, August 24, 1978, between the mayor (far right), and political adversary Council President George Forbes (left). Joining the two men, who dined on eggs and grits, were their wives, Mary and Sandy.

(Right) CONGRATULATING THE NEW MAYOR, November 6, 1979

Press columnist Dick Feagler wrote on Wednesday, November 7, 1979, "The town was a hit man yesterday. It terminated Dennis Kucinich with extreme prejudice," after Republican challenger George V. Voinovich (right), the state's lieutenant governor, defeated the feisty 33-year-old in the mayoral election. After conceding the election on election night, Kucinich (left), who carried only eight of the city's 33 wards, visited the mayor-elect at his Cleveland Plaza Hotel campaign headquarters where he offered his congratulations. Voinovich became the city's first mayor in nearly 20 years to capture a majority of both black and white votes. Among the new mayor's first tasks were moving to end the city's default, beginning the search for a new finance director and appointing a new police chief.

Section I
The War Years

**AT THE STANDARD DRUG STORE,
E. NINTH & SUPERIOR
August 10, 1945**

Standard Drug employees Ethel Fisher
(left), Helen Wildman and Sandra
Baron celebrate news of Japan's offer
to surrender on Friday, August 10, 1945.

BOB FELLER RETURNS TO THE INDIANS, 1945

Local heavyweight Jimmy Bivins was scheduled to fight Archie Moore at Municipal Stadium on Wednesday, August 22, 1945, the night Cleveland Indians ace Bob Feller (above center), was released from military service. At the time, only six members of the Indians squad he left in 1941 remained on the current roster- player-manager Lou Boudreau, Jeff Heath, Mel Harder, Al Smith, Gene Desautels and Jim Bagby. On Friday, August 24th, Feller was honored at a Hotel Carter luncheon before pitching his first game that evening, a 6-5, complete-game win over starter Hal Newhouser and the Detroit Tigers before 46,000 at the Stadium. **(Above right)** Folks stand in line to purchase

tickets at Bond's Men's Store for the August 24th game.

(Left) Feller appears before the game on August 24th with former Cleveland player-manager and Hall of Famer Tris Speaker in his new Jeep, one of many gifts he received.

The Cleveland Press Roll of Honor

As the Shaw High Band played in the background, hundreds of mothers, fathers and wives waited patiently to place the names of their loved servicemen and women in the massive book, when the 250-page Greater Cleveland Roll of Honor was opened for inscription in front of The Press Building on Wednesday, May 6, 1942. Over 1,000 names were inscribed in the book, covered in rich blue leather with its gold-letter cover and red, white and blue pages, by the end of the first day. After the first day of inscription, the book was placed in The Press Building lobby where Americans from all walks of life added names to the public record.

(Above right) After addressing the crowd during the opening ceremonies, Mayor Frank Lausche became the first dignitary to inscribe his name on the Roll of Honor. Mrs. Robert Horowitz, who had waited in line since 7 A.M., was first to enter a name in the guest registrant's column.

(Right) Among the many celebrities signing the book were Helen Hayes, Jan Struthers, author of the novel, "Mrs. Minniver," and selective service director General Lewis Hershey. At right, actress Ilona Massey signs the Roll of Honor on Monday, September 14, 1942, as actors Fred Astaire and Hugh Herbert look on. After headlining a Navy War Bond rally at Public Hall the night before, the three stars appeared at a War Bond luncheon that after-noon at Hotel Statler where a pair of white tap-dancing shoes worn by Astaire while filming "Holiday Inn," raised $116,000 in War Bond sales.

Up to 3,000 area men were scheduled to depart for military duty over the upcoming week, when the patriotic parade at left was conducted on Saturday, September 15, 1917. Five divisions of selective servicemen, one division of military organizations, and a division composed of prominent citizens, joined nine marching bands for the 2 P.M. parade down Euclid Avenue to Public Square. Over 4,000 men marched past thousands of well-wishers before passing the reviewing stand built on the east side of Soldiers and Sailors monument.

(Below) Men from Districts 2 and 3 prepare to head out for Camp Sherman from the city's Erie Street station on Wednesday, September 19, 1917. As friends and families said their goodbyes from the station, most of the 1,830 leaving for military training "went gay and laughing, waiving their hats and yelling farewells from the departing trains."

World War I
Leaving to Fight the Kaiser
September, 1917

HEADING OFF TO MEXICO, June 23, 1916

"Figures Friday showed 647 men are needed to fill ranks of Cleveland's O. N. G. for service in Mexico," reported The Press on Friday, June 23, 1916. The next day, hoping to call attention to the need for volunteers, over 1,150 guardsmen of Cleveland's O. N. G., including the Cleveland Grays, marched along downtown streets (right), after massing at Central Armory.

(Right) RECRUITING NEW MARINES, August 8, 1917

The countywide search for new Marine recruits received a boost on Wednesday, August 8, 1917, when the new vehicle at right arrived from Buffalo. Posing in front of the new recruiting weapon were Lieut. I. J. Logan (left), Assistant Surgeon R. P. Bell and sergeants R. J. Rutgen (inside car), H. W. Schwab, H. F. Drakins, J. J. Murphy, P. J. Schmid and A. Harden (right).

GEN. JOHN J. PERSHING COMES TO TOWN ARMISTICE DAY, 1927

Reporter David Dietz wrote in The Press on Friday, November 11, 1927, "A plea for world peace by the soldier who led America's forces to victory in the World War climaxed Cleveland's celebration of the ninth anniversary of Armistice Day." The peace plea came at the end of remarks made at Public Hall by Gen. John J. (Black Jack) Pershing who arrived by train early that morning. After eating breakfast at the home of Samuel Mather, Pershing (immediately behind the mounted brigade at left), was escorted along Euclid Ave. to Public Hall by a parade group that included the Cleveland Grays and Troop A of the 107th Cavalry O. N. G. at left. Pershing's Public Hall remarks were broadcast to the nation on a Blue Network program originating through WEAR and WTAM radio stations.

(Left)
ALONG EUCLID AVENUE

At 7 P.M. Eastern war time on Tuesday, August 14, 1945, President Harry S. Truman signaled the end of World War II by announcing that Japan had agreed to Allied terms. Within minutes of receiving the joyous news, celebrants jammed Euclid Avenue bringing traffic to a standstill. Confetti and paper streamers swirled from windows along Euclid as many motorists left their autos to party in the street.

(Left, Below left, Bottom left)
Clevelanders celebrate at the corner of Euclid Avenue and E. Ninth St. around 8:15 P.M. on August 14th. A policeman stationed at the intersection during the first half hour remarked, "I didn't expect it to blow up so quickly." The lives of over 3,378 local servicemen were lost in the global conflict.

Celebrating the End of World War II,

August 14, 1945

(Right) Bartender Eddie Zeitz puts out the closed sign at Church's Grill in Lakewood. When word of Japan's surrender reached the city, Mayor Thomas A. Burke called Police Chief George J. Matowitz who immediately put the city's entire police force into action, cancelling furloughs and days off. Downtown Cleveland bars were forced to close at 7 P.M. on August 14th, as police began chasing out customers. By 8 P.M., it was almost impossible to buy a drink downtown.

(Right) Though a heavy rainstorm hit the city at 9:25 P.M. on August 14th, it failed to dampen the victory party as thousands crowded onto downtown streets. At right, revelers packed Public Square near the W. B. Davis Co. store on Euclid Ave., where the celebration carried on into the early morning hours. A survey of local companies found that while the big dairy companies would be delivering milk the next morning, most other stores would be closed on the 15th, a national holiday.

(Below) Toasting the end of World War II at the Spaghetti Inn, 6820 Wade Park Ave.

(Below right) Housewives and their children celebrating the news outside 415 Gladys Ave. in Lakewood.

At The Cleveland Press

"Japs To Get Terms at Manila- U. S. Ends Gas Rations- Canned Fruit, Fuel Oil, Stoves also released;" "$350,000 in Contracts Cancelled in Cleveland Area;" "Truman to See Newsmen;" and "U. S. Celebrates War End, Hirohito Gives Japs News;" were some of the front page headlines found in the special "Victory Edition" of The Cleveland Press on Wednesday, August 15, 1945. At right, Clevelanders scramble for the first copies of the "Victory Edition" in The Press Building lobby Wednesday morning. The word "Peace" was printed in huge red, white and blue letters across the front page.

The War Bond Parade
January 20, 1944

"Uncle Sam staged a deadly looking "fashion parade," in Cleveland today," wrote Cleveland Press reporter Noel Wical following the noon parade at left on Thursday, January 20, 1944. Sponsored by the Retail Merchants' Board, the parade saluted the Army as the city kicked off its 4th War Loan Bond drive. Featured in the parade were marching units, several bands and a number of "Axis-hammering" mobile guns including a 40-millimeter Bofors anti-aircraft gun; a 105-millimeter howitzer with a seven-mile range; a 57-millimeter anti-tank gun and 'Long Tom,' a 15-ton, 150-millimeter gun.

Capt. Don Gentile Day

As area residents were being urged to buy War Bonds during the Fifth War Loan Drive beginning the next day, on Sunday, June 11, 1944, over 25,000 spectators cheering "Don, Don," lined Euclid Avenue to see Capt. Don Gentile (right), the top-ranking American fighter pilot in the European theater. With the handsome airman from Piqua, OH were mayor Frank J. Lausche (left); his fiancee, Miss Isabella Masdea of Columbus, OH; and his mother Mrs. Josephine Gentile. After the parade, Gentile was driven to the Sons of Italy Hall where mothers of Italian servicemen were honored. Afterward, Gentile attended a banquet at Hotel Cleveland. The Cleveland Kiltie Band, the Russo Band and a detachment of Waves with color guard were among the groups joining over 1,000 citizens, military personnel and veterans led by Mounted Troop A of the Cleveland Police, who marched with Gentile from Public Square to Playhouse Square.

Sunday, June 11, 1944

(Far left) On Monday, June 12, 1944, Capt. Don Gentile, credited with shooting down 30 Nazi planes, received a $1,000 War Bond in the name of the people of Cleveland from Ugo Carusi, executive assistant of the U. S. attorney general. Behind the men is Gentile's father. Upon arriving in town for a three-day stay on June 10th, Gentile visited injured soldiers at Crile General Hospital and was honored that night by the Sons of Italy at a banquet held at Chef Boiardi's restaurant. Later that night, Gentile appeared on stage with bandleader Guy Lombardo at the RKO Palace.

(Above) MARLENE DIETRICH, May 13, 1942

Before performing with Al Jolson in "Command Performance," at the National Association of Broadcasters banquet in Hotel Carter, Hollywood star Marlene Dietrich, above with Kenny Baker, took time from her hectic schedule on Wednesday, May 13, 1942, to visit three hospitals, Marine, Veterans and Sunny Acres; and greet soldiers heading off to war at Union Terminal.

(Below) GLENN MILLER, October 25, 1943

Mayor Frank J. Lausche (second left), joins Mrs. Mark W. Clark, wife of the Commanding General of America's 5th Army and band leader Capt. Glenn Miller (left), on Monday, October 25, 1943. Clark and Miller were in town for the opening of the four-day May Company Four Freedoms War Bond Show.

The Hollywood Bond Cavalcade

The city's Third War Loan Bond Drive was $83,702,000 richer on Sunday, September 12, 1943, after an appearance by the star-studded Hollywood Cavalcade.

(Right) Band leader Kay Kyser sells War Bonds at a Hotel Carter luncheon before the Cavalcade show. The luncheon raised $60,380,000 in bond sales. Kyser's 24-piece band provided music for the Public Hall show led by Mickey Rooney that night, where $23,322,000 was raised during the show attended by 10,665.

(Far right) Kyser with Harpo Marx.

(Right) Cavalcade members pose after arriving in the city. (Standing L-R): Judy Garland, Paul Henreid, Lucille Ball, Eddie Buzzell, Katherine Grayson, Harpo Marx, Greer Garson, Jane Lausche, Fred Astaire, Betty Hutton, Diana Pendleton. (Bottom L-R): Harry Babbitt, Ish Kabibble, Ruth Brady, Muriel Goodspeed, Rosemary La Plauche, Mickey Rooney, Marjorie Stewart, Doris Merrick and Julia Conway. Among the missing were Dick Powell and Jimmy Cagney.

September 12, 1943

Section J
Police & Fire

August 6, 1933

Wearing their new white pith helmets, Troop A officers move out to participate in the Fraternal Order of Eagles parade along Euclid Avenue on Sunday, August 6, 1933. Led by a squad of motorcycle policeman followed by the mounted troops below left, over 7,000 marchers paraded along the main thoroughfare to the Eagles Club at 4705 Euclid. The colorful procession served as a climax to the organization's 35th annual national convention in Cleveland.

On Mounted Patrol

(Left) **PERFORMING AT THE SUMMER OPERA FESTIVAL, July 28, 1931**

A six-night Summer Opera Festival was one of the first events staged at the city's newly-opened Municipal Stadium along the lakefront. As the open-air festival readied for opening night on Tuesday, July 28, 1931, The Press reported, "Through the efforts of Safety Director Edwin D. Barry (front center), Cleveland's finest horses will be there in formation, putting the finishing touch to a magnificent picture." **(Left)** Members of Troops A, B, and C go through a final dress rehearsal on July 27th, under the review of Barry and Police Chief George J. Matowitz. The horses were used in the second scene of "Aida," viewed by 18,064, an open-air opera record.

(Right)
THE CITY'S NEW HORSES, July 11, 1940

According to The Press on Thursday, July 11, 1940, the Cleveland Police Department paid $2,865 for fourteen four to five-year-old horses, all 16 hands high and weighing between 1,150 to 1,200 pounds. "I've never seen a finer lot of hillbillies before in my 28 years with the troop," Big Jim Matowitz, brother of Chief George J. Matowitz, told the newspaper. Matowitz, in charge of the Troop A stables at E. 13th and Rockwell added, "They are all from registered Kentucky saddle horse stock. In another week or two they'll be all set to perform their duties." The new additions brought the mounted division to its full strength of 44 horses. At right, Patrolman James Halloran (left), Patrolman Fred Kneiss, Patrolman William Carter and Patrolman Raymond Lynch (right), put four of the newly-purchased horses through their paces.

On Motorcycle Patrol

(Left) THE CITY'S NEW MOTORCYCLES, September 21, 1938

"These motor cops 'll get you if you don't watch out," reported The Press on Wednesday, September 21, 1938. The paper continued, "Each member of the police "suicide squad"- the motorcycle traffic officers-had individual cycles today after the city purchased 27 new Harley-Davidsons." Joining his officers at far right is Police Chief George J. Matowitz.

(Right) THE CITY'S NEW MOTORCYCLE SQUAD, April 25, 1958

On Friday, April 25, 1958, the city's new 13-member motorcycle squad, unofficially nicknamed "The Marauders," took to city streets on their new $1,500 Harley-Davidson motorcycles. Led by Sgt. Hans Tonne (far right), each officer received an extra $120 a year for cycle duty.

(Right) ANNUAL PARADE DAY FOR CITY DEPARTMENTS, June 28, 1919

"Both Fire and Police Departments make an increasingly impressive appearance each year, and won popular commendation from those who saw them Saturday," reported The Press on Saturday, June 28, 1919, after the city held its annual Parade Day for city departments. The city's men in uniform marched from E. 40th St. to Public Square buoyed by the knowledge that the front page of The Press proclaimed in large bold letters, "Germany Signs; War Is Over." Leading the policemen at right along Euclid Avenue was Police Chief Frank W. Smith. During the festivities, city officials awarded patrolman Patrick McNeeley the Police Department's Gold Medal for 1918. McNeeley received the medal for capturing two burglars "at the risk of life" in July of 1918.

Our Men in Blue

(Left) TRAFFIC COMMISSIONER "SILVER EDDIE" DONAHUE IS LAID TO REST, July 17, 1939

E. Ninth Street was closed to traffic on Monday, July 17, 1939, as thousands paid their last respects to Edward J. Donahue at St. John Cathedral. Donahue, described as "a genial, rosy-cheeked Irishman," served 15 years as Cleveland's first traffic commissioner, developing a system of traffic regulation regarded as a model plan at the time. His first act was to install red and green lights at major intersections. Donahue once described his early days as a patrolman in the old "Roaring Third" Precinct, to The Press saying, "Those were grand days. We sometimes had to climb up ladders into dark attics looking for gunmen and trust against our better judgment that we'd come out alive. We wanted to do all the capturing ourselves and got sore if the detectives butted in." He was buried at Calvary Cemetery.

(Below left) NEW RECRUITS, NEW UNIFORMS, March 9, 1942

"All new, from uniforms to training, these 33 additions to the Cleveland Police Department went on duty today," The Press reported on Monday, March 9, 1942. The new officers joining Academy officials are: (left-right, front row): Mac Griesmar, Fifth District; Orville Dew, Accident Prevention Bureau; Thomas Garrity, First District; William Hudec, Fourth District; Henry Abel, Fifth District; Richard Cook, Fourth District; Frank Lensaric, Accident Prevention Bureau; Dean of the Cleveland Police Academy Inspector Patrick Lenahan. (second row): Frank Cawthra, Second District; Ray Mlarkar, Second District; Anton Lohn, First District; William Brady, Third District; Joseph Kocher, Accident Prevention Bureau; James Orenski, Fifth District; Harry Weitzel, Third District. (third row): John Golden, Fifth District; Edward Gordon, Fifth District; Charles Sullivan, First District; Henry Cavanagh, Accident Prevention Bureau; Stephen Radachy, Fourth District; Peter Skirbunt, Fourth District. (fourth row): Secretary of Police James Livingston; Richard Duncan, Third District; Fred O'Malley, Third District; and Joseph Colan, Accident Prevention Bureau.

(Right) SPOILING A HOLDUP, November 1, 1957

Gas station attendant Richard Whelpley, 20, salutes Cleveland Patrolmen Tony Karnowski and Al Rocco on Friday, November 1, 1957, after the two officers broke up a holdup at the gas station where Whelpley worked. Early that morning, Karnowski and Rocco were checking the Sohio station at E. 46th Street where Carnegie and Prospect meet, when they saw a man pointing a gun at a customer who had brought his car in to be greased. With guns drawn, the officers peacefully apprehended the gunman and then rescued Whelpley, a father of two, who had been locked in a storage room.

(Below) THE COFFEE PATROL, December 30, 1961

As the city prepared to enter the new year on Saturday, December 30, 1961, Harvey's Oak Room teamed up with the Public Relations Department of the Cleveland Police to provide free coffee packets to

downtown motorists on the 30th and 31st. **(Left)** Oak Room waitress Miss Brigitte Karolyi hands a coffee packet to a waiting motorist. She was scheduled to provide brewed coffee until "uncooperative temperatures chilled the idea and the coffee." The free coffee message was broadcast to motorists over the police wagon's loudspeakers.

(Right) THE MAN FROM "U.N.C.L.E.", February 23, 1965

"As a Press reporter, I escorted blond, Beatle-haired McCallum through Central Police Station," wrote Judy Prusnek (on desk), on Tuesday, February 23, 1965, after spending time with 30-year-old Scottish actor David McCallum, co-star of NBC-TV's, "The Man From U.N.C.L.E." **(Right)** Scientific Investigation Unit Sgt. Lee Peters administers a polygraph test to McCallum, who played Iilya, the Russian-born master spy, during his tour.

THE INAUGURAL POLICE AND FIRE FIELD DAY, September 11, 1933

Hoping to raise money for new uniforms, the first annual Police and Firemen's Field Day was held at Municipal Stadium on Sunday, September 11, 1933. Though the fire department squad captured the baseball game, 4-0; the pre-meet underdogs of Police Chief George J. Matowitz captured the tug-of-war and the Field Day trophy, easily beating Fire Chief James E. Granger's squad, 79-57, before 51,308 at the Stadium. In addition to track events, an obstacle race and boxing matches, a number of exhibitions were presented including calisthenics and stunt riding on horses and motorcycles. East Tech track star Jesse Owens won the AAU 100-meter dash for men.

(Right) A scene from the opening ceremonies. The tower was used to demonstrate fire-fighting techniques including leaping into nets.

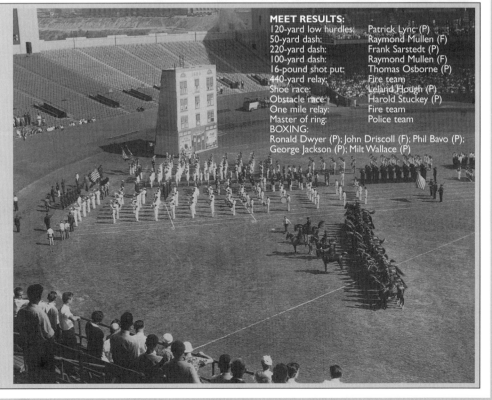

MEET RESULTS:

120-yard low hurdles:	Patrick Lync (P)
50-yard dash:	Raymond Mullen (F)
220-yard dash:	Frank Sarstedt (P)
100-yard dash:	Raymond Mullen (F)
16-pound shot put:	Thomas Osborne (P)
440-yard relay:	Fire team
Shoe race:	Leland Hough (P)
Obstacle race:	Harold Stuckey (P)
One mile relay:	Fire team
Master of ring:	Police team

BOXING:
Ronald Dwyer (P); John Driscoll (F); Phil Bavo (P); George Jackson (P); Milt Wallace (P)

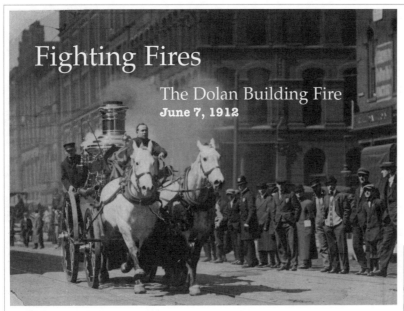

Fighting Fires

The Dolan Building Fire
June 7, 1912

The total loss, fixed at $70,500, was covered by insurance, reported The Press on Saturday, June 8, 1912, after fire in the attic of the Dolan Building at 238-40 Superior Avenue threatened to destroy a row of office buildings between Euclid and Superior. The fire, which began around midnight Friday evening, "was raging on the fifth floor, occupied by the Volk gymnasium, when Patrolman Woodring turned in the alarm," according to the paper. Damages were reported as follows: Building, owned by Samuel Keller, $20,000; Dolan Co. clothiers, who occupied the first, second, third and fourth floors, $30,000; Maple lunch room, second floor, owned by H. D. Jones, $3,500; Volk gymnasium, fifth floor, $5,000; damage to surrounding offices and stores, $12,000.

(Above) One of the city's aging two-horse steam engines racing to the Dolan Building fire. **(Right)** The firemen at right returned to fighting the fire after narrowly escaping injury when the building's roof caved in. The firemen were called out of the building only moments before the roof collapsed. "Second and third alarms however, brought sufficient apparatus to confine the flames to the upper floors," The Press reported.

(Left) THE CITY'S FIRST AUTO FIRE ENGINE, December 16, 1912

"When the city's new fire house at Ashbury and E. 122nd opened for service on Monday, the proudest man in the department was Carl Patterson. For Pat, member of the department for 19 years to the hour, sat at the wheel of Cleveland's first auto fire engine," reported The Press on Monday, December 16, 1912. The new seven-ton fire engine, purchased for $7,250, was a four-cylinder, 75-horsepower machine with a top speed of 40 miles an hour. Its electric pumps were capable of throwing 700 gallons of water a minute through its 1,000 feet of hose. "With the horse-drawn steamer, 18 miles an hour on a short run is about the limit," Patterson reported. "Of course I'm sorry in a way to see the horses go, But its hard on them, even though they're well cared for. I've seen horses drop in the harness and bleed at the mouth after a hard run. Their feet are pounded to pieces on the pavement."

THE EARLIEST AND THE LATEST, February 13, 1929

"Back in the days before women had legs, when 12 miles an hour was breakneck speed, when folks

traveled about Ohio in stage coaches and Morse was tinkering with a thing he called a telegraph, the City of Cleveland acquired a fine new fire engine," offered The Press on Wednesday, February 13, 1929. Upper left is the original hand-drawn hand pumper the city of 17,000 purchased from a Philadelphia manufacturer in 1843. It took eight men to operate the "scientific fire apparatus" which shot a stream of water "fully 25 feet in length" from its leather hose. The pumper was purchased from the city in 1916 for $200 by a group of Lorain County firemen. **(Upper right)** One of the department's newest fire fighting pieces in 1929.

(Above) RAISING A NEW FLAG, July 9, 1943

"Setting an example that they hope will be followed by other neighborhood groups, the Shadyside Exchange Club, an organization of business and professional groups from the W. 25th- Clark Avenue areas has presented Hook and Ladder Company No. 5 of the fire department with a new flag," The Press reported on Friday, July 9, 1943. Above, Company No. 5 firemen stand at attention as Sgt. Edward Monigle of the U. S. Marine recruiting office raises the newly-accepted flag.

(Below) SPREADING THE HOLIDAY SPIRIT AT STATION NO. 9, December 19, 1956

"Turned toy surgeons in their idle hours are Cleveland fireman whose holiday labors will bring much happiness to children for whom Santa would otherwise have little meaning," offered The Press on Wednesday, December 19, 1956. Below, firemen William Billups (left), Lieut. George Oravec, Eugene Guyton and Robert Temansky (right), work on holiday gifts for area youth at Station No. 9, E. 68th and Woodland Avenue.

(Right, Below Right) THE GILLSY HOTEL FIRE, December 30, 1952

Shortly before noon on Tuesday, December 30, 1952, one of the most spectacular downtown fires in several years broke out at the Gillsy Hotel, 1811 E. Ninth, forcing the evacuation of nearly 300 patrons, including most of the cast appearing at the Roxy Burlesque across the street. "All reached safety without injury, including Crystal Wade (inset), a dancer, and Bert Schmelzer, candy butcher in the Roxy Theater, who were briefly trapped in a room on the top floor," reported The Press. "I was sleeping in my room on the 10th floor when the cry of fire came, but by the time I'd put on bra and panties, I got scared," said Wade. "Somewhere I found a man's topcoat and shoes, and put them on. I don't know where I got them and I never had time to find my own clothes in the smoke and water. I only saved a blonde wig I use in the show. But any way you look at it. I guess this is my lucky day." At right, smoke curls out of the eighth floor as thousands gathered below to watch the drama unfold. Wade and Schmelzer can be seen looking out the window a floor above the ladder. Fire Chief Elmer Cain placed the damage at $10,000.

(Below right) AT CHAGRIN AND LEE, May 5, 1966

The cause was still undetermined on Thursday, May 5, 1966, after fire swept through five stores (right), at Chagrin Blvd. and Lee Rd. on May 4th. Fire Chief George L. Vild estimated the damage to be "in the $350,000 class," making the blaze the most costly in Shaker Heights' history at the time.

(Left) ACCEPTING THE POSITION, 1935

On Wednesday, December 11, 1935, Mayor Harold Hitz Burton (left), swore in 32-year-old Eliot H. Ness, boyish looking head of the Federal Government's liquor tax enforcement in the northern half of Ohio, as the city's new safety director. Despite strong opposition from within the police and fire departments and from organized labor, on November 13, 1941, mayor Frank Lausche, a newly-elected Democrat, crossed party lines to retain Ness, a Republican, in the city's safety post. On Monday, April 27, 1942, as Ness was leaving his Cleveland job for a Federal post in Washington, D.C., Press reporter Clayton Fritchey wrote, "Most people will agree it (Cleveland) is a much better place."

AS SAFETY DIRECTOR, 1936 and 1938

(Above) Ness leads a group of investigators interrogating area hobos near Kingsbury Run on Tuesday, August 16, 1938, after the remains of torso murders 11 and 12 were discovered.

Eliot Ness as Cleveland's Safety Director

(Left) "An order to drive out of the city six gamblers who long have operated the Thomas and Harvard clubs was given today by Safety Director Eliot Ness," reported The Press on Saturday, January 11, 1936, after police raided the Harvard Club the night before. Ness (second, right), confers with the raiding party led by County Prosecutor Frank T. Cullitan. Ness issued the order after machine gun fire held the raiders at bay for six hours while the club was stripped of its gambling paraphernalia.

Running for Mayor, 1947

In 1947, Ness, at age 44, returned to Cleveland after a five-year absence, to oppose incumbent mayor Thomas A. Burke as an "independent" candidate with Republican support. Burke soundly defeated Ness by an 82,422 vote margin in the November election. Ness later moved to Pennsylvania where he authored a book about his legendary exploits. Unfortunately, Ness died of a heart attack on May 19, 1957, only weeks before his book, "The Untouchables," was published.

(Left, Above) Ness hits the campaign trail in August of 1947 with his third wife Elizabeth, the former Mrs. Hugh Seaver, an accomplished New York sculptress. When he announced his candidacy on Wednesday, July 30, 1947, Ness told reporters, "When I left Cleveland five years ago to enter the war program, Cleveland was a vibrant, spirited city, interested in accomplishment and improvement. I returned to find it, by comparison, a tired and listless town; its air filled with soot and smoke; its streets dirty and in a most deplorable condition, its transportation system noisy, inadequate and approaching insolvency."

(Left) VICTIM NUMBER SIX, September 10, 1936

When efforts by the investigators at left failed to provide any clues on Thursday, September 10, 1936, divers were brought in to search the murky waters for the head and limbs missing from the torso murderer's sixth victim. Press reporter William Miller began his story in the paper on September 11th with, "Last midnight, I went down to Kingsbury Run. Kingsbury Run, that mysterious gully where prowls a mad butcher. Four of his headless victims have been found there. He has killed two others."

VICTIMS ELEVEN AND TWELVE, August 17, 1938

After new bones of victim 11, reportedly a man between 40 and 50, were discovered in a lake front dump along Shore Drive east of E. Ninth Street on Wednesday, August 17, 1938, the front page story in The Press began, "This Torso Killer, What Sort of Madman is He? A cunning madman with the strength of an ox. That's the torso killer- the murderer who has ruthlessly slain 12 men and women, then dismembered their bodies and hidden the parts in lonely places. He's as regular, as coldly efficient and as relentless as an executioner when the mood to kill comes over him."

(Below left) Coroner Samuel R. Gerber digs for the remains of torso victims at the dump with Det. Sgt. James Hogan and Deputy Police Inspector Charles O. Nevel on August 17th. The bones of victim 12, a blonde woman

The Kingsbury Run Torso Murders

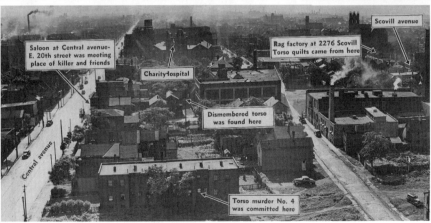

Saloon at Central avenue-
E. 20th street was meeting
place of killer and friends

Charity Hospital

Scovill avenue

Rag factory at 2276 Scovill
Torso quilts came from here

Dismembered torso
was found here

Central avenue

Torso murder No. 4
was committed here

about 35-years-old, were discovered nearby bones of victim 11 the previous day. The bones were found by men rummaging through the dump. (Above) A shantytown inhabited by 59 hobos near the main investigation area was searched for clues on Thursday, August 18, 1938, and then set afire by the Cleveland Fire Department. The transients were arrested and taken to Central Station. A total of twelve dismembered bodies were found between September of 1935 and August of 1938. The murderer was never found.

FRANK DOLEZAL CONFESSES TO MURDER #3, July 7, 1939

On Friday, July 7, 1939, Sheriff Martin L. O'Donnell announced that he had obtained a signed confession from 52-year-old bricklayer Frank Dolezal, who admitted to dismembering the body of victim number three, found in the Kingsbury run area on January 26, 1936. Though there were several holes in Dolezal's testimony, O'Donnell said he had no doubt that Dolezal was "the mad butcher of Kingsbury Run." By Tuesday, July 11, 1936, questions about Dolezal's guilt were being raised by a number of sources including The Press, who asked, "Is Frank Dolezal the torso murderer? Or is he a harmless psychopath who has been forced into a crime he did not commit?" Dolezal, who was suspected of being brutally beaten while in custody, hung himself in County Jail on August 24th before being cleared of the crime.
(Above) An aerial view of how Dolezal's former home at 1908 Central Avenue put him in the midst of the crime scene. (Right) Dolezal with Assistant County Detective Joseph Krupansky after being brought in for questioning.

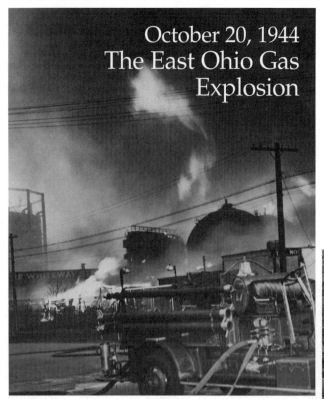

October 20, 1944
The East Ohio Gas Explosion

On Monday, December 2, 1940, The Press printed the aerial photo below showing the East Ohio Gas Company's three new tanks under construction at E. 61st Street. According to the paper, the tanks being built were the world's first large tanks designed to house liquefied gas, with each tank capable of holding 50,000,000 cubic feet of gas. At 2:40 P.M. on Friday, October 20, 1944, the small tank under construction below mysteriously exploded, creating a horrifying fireball that devastated a half-mile square area surrounding the tanks. The danger of additional explosions forced the evacuation of more than 10,000 residents from the area bounded by St. Clair Avenue N.E., E. 55th St., E. 67th St., and Memorial Shoreway. Coroner Samuel Gerber tagged 130 bodies at the scene, but only 77 had been positively identified two months later. Over 250 homes were destroyed, leaving some 2,000 homeless. "We saw a big balloon of fire spreading over the whole neighborhood. Fire was everywhere," said a nearby Fisher-Babcock Co. worker after the explosion converted

the storage plant into a gigantic flame thrower with flames shooting an estimated 2,800 feet in the air. "We heard the blast, then the entire neighborhood rocked," said another observer. A total of six separate explosions were reported at the gas plant coupled with twenty or more explosions of nearby gas mains and manhole covers, some covers spiraling several hundred feet in the air. That night, with electricity

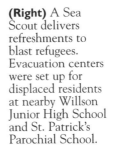

(Right) A Sea Scout delivers refreshments to blast refugees. Evacuation centers were set up for displaced residents at nearby Willson Junior High School and St. Patrick's Parochial School.

cut off to the area, volunteers were forced to search for missing persons by lantern light.

(Top) Workers who stated, "somebody's got to do it," began draining the two remaining liquid gas tanks on Monday, October 23, 1944.

(Above left) The tremendous explosion on October 20th consumed hundreds of homes and small stores. By Sunday, October 22nd, Fire Chief James E. Granger had placed the damage at $7,000,000.

(Above) Kenneth H. Donaldson (left), George E. Barnes, Matthew M. Braidech, Carl F. Prutton, councilmen Edward Kovacic and Edward L. Pucel, James H. Herron and safety director Frank D. Celebreeze (right), were members of the 10-man board of inquiry Mayor Frank J. Lausche appointed to investigate the tragic event, one of the city's worst disasters.

(Above middle) Within hours of the blast, nearly 3,000 policemen, civilian defense workers, doctors, nurses, military police and members of all the armed services were helping restore order and provide emergency relief services to the district.

(Above) The remains of 61 unidentified victims were buried in a memorial service conducted by clergy of three faiths at Highland Park Cemetery on Tuesday, November 14, 1944.

(Left, Right) Youngsters at play at the blast site on Wednesday, September 18, 1946. Councilmen Edward Kovacic and Anton Grdina were among local leaders working to turn the land into a community park.

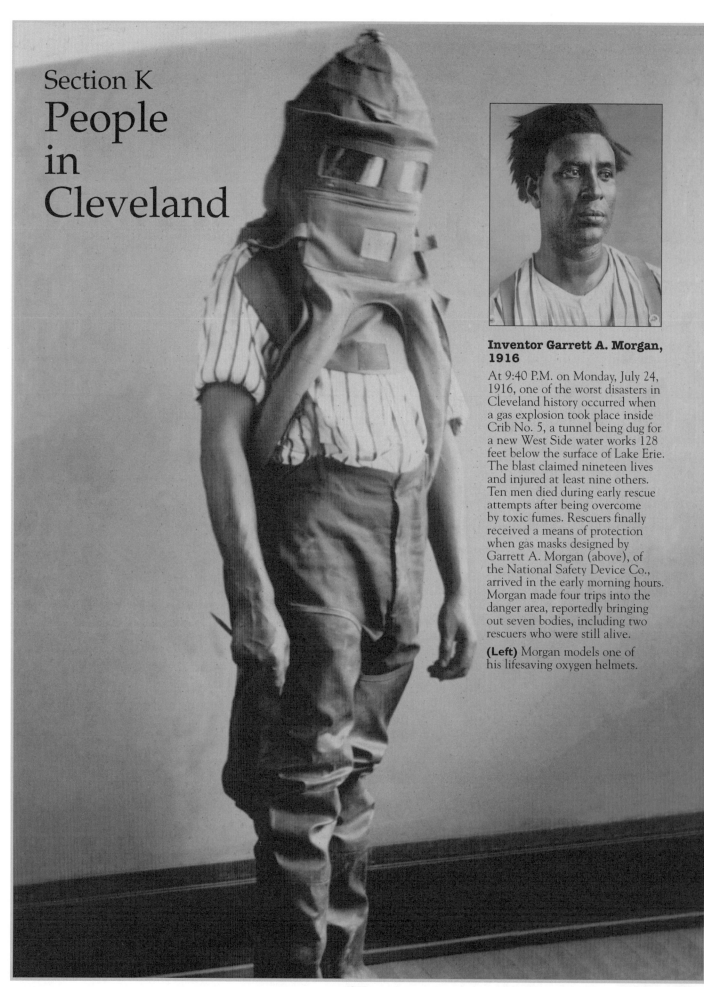

Section K
People in Cleveland

Inventor Garrett A. Morgan, 1916

At 9:40 P.M. on Monday, July 24, 1916, one of the worst disasters in Cleveland history occurred when a gas explosion took place inside Crib No. 5, a tunnel being dug for a new West Side water works 128 feet below the surface of Lake Erie. The blast claimed nineteen lives and injured at least nine others. Ten men died during early rescue attempts after being overcome by toxic fumes. Rescuers finally received a means of protection when gas masks designed by Garrett A. Morgan (above), of the National Safety Device Co., arrived in the early morning hours. Morgan made four trips into the danger area, reportedly bringing out seven bodies, including two rescuers who were still alive.

(Left) Morgan models one of his lifesaving oxygen helmets.

(**Above**) Olympic champion Jesse Owens and his wife, Ruth Solomon Owens, are surrounded by well wishers at the train station after returning to Cleveland from the Olympic Games in Berlin, Germany where Jesse won four gold medals.

Cleveland's Jesse Owens Returns Home After Winning Olympic Gold

(**Above right**) On Monday, August 24, 1936, after returning to New York from Germany on the Queen Mary, 21-year-old Jesse Owens was entertained by tap dancer Bill Robinson in Robinson's Harlem apartment before heading back to Cleveland that evening. Owens arrived at the East Cleveland New York Central station (above right), at 8:15 A.M. where over 2,500 waited for the track and field star to arrive.

(**Right**) With Jesse as he left the East Cleveland station at 9 A.M. were Councilman Henry Finkle (left), local boxing commissioner and parade organizer Tris Speaker (center, rear), Lieut. Governor Harold Mosier (center, front), Mrs. Ruth Owens, Jesse's wife and Mayor Harold Burton. Thousands lined city streets from E. 55th to W. 25th to see Cleveland's newest hero during Jesse's 13-mile trek to Public Hall, where he was welcomed by more than 4,000. Owens later toured the Great Lakes Exposition.

August 25, 1936

WITH HOLLIDAY AND BLOSSOM, DECEMBER 6, 1936 Based on the success of the Great Lakes Exposition in 1936,

A. C. Ernst

which brought nearly four million summertime visitors to the city during its 108-day run, plans for a 1937 edition of the lakefront extravaganza were put in motion on Sunday, December 6, 1936, when civic leaders met at Hotel Statler to organize a $500,000 fund raising campaign. At far left, Great Lakes Exposition vice president A. C. Ernst (right), managing partner of accounting firm Ernst & Ernst, discusses Exposition plans on December 6th with newly-elected Expo president W. T. Holliday, president of Standard Oil Co. of Ohio (left), and Expo general chairman Dudley S. Blossom. More than $300,000 had already been raised.

(**Left**) **WITH LOUIS B. SELTZER, 1945** Created to place a fountain on the Mall, the $100,000 Press Memorial Fountain Fund campaign received a major boost on Friday, June 1, 1945, when A. C. Ernst presented a $2,500 check to Press Editor Louis B. Seltzer.

Some Famous...

(Above) THE RED CROSS WEEK CAMPAIGN COMMITTEE, June 16, 1917

"The Red Cross will face the task of caring for the hundreds of thousands of soldiers America will send to France," The Press declared on Saturday, June 16, 1917, as the city began a one-week campaign to raise $2,500,000 for Red Cross relief work during World War I. Among the local leaders spearheading the effort were William G. Mather (left), Fred H. Goff, Paul L. Feiss, committee chairman Samuel Mather, Myron T. Herrick, M. B. Johnson and Warren S. Hayden (right).

Stella Walsh

(Below) THE RESTAURATEURS, April 16, 1948

Local restaurateur Hector (Chef) Boiardi (below left), "the spaghetti king," helps fellow restaurant owner, and partner, Frank Monaco, unpack chairs prior to the opening of Monaco's new restaurant in the former Allendorf Restaurant site at 1116 Chester Avenue. "It was an evening of triumphs for Frank Monaco," reported a local paper after a special gala for media and City Hall representatives was held at his new night spot on Friday, April 16, 1948. Johnny Huntington's orchestra played at the sold-out premiere, offering sweet melodies from the balcony as Pinky Hunter of WHK Radio introduced first-nighters in a live broadcast from the room. The 400-seat restaurant featured an intimate lounge, an oak-lined private room, a limed-oak barroom and one of the city's swankiest dining rooms, "smartly ultra-modernistic in a restful eye-appealing fashion." Monaco returned to the local scene after selling his popular cafe in the Hanna Building several years earlier.

Hector Boiardi

Frank Monaco

(Above) STELLA WALSH, June 27, 1947 Stella Walsh (top row center), the city's world-record-setting track standout, joined Polish Olympic Athletic Club teammates Eleanor Repinski; Bessie Leick; (middle row): Jean Walraven; Frances Kaszubski; Marion Kachelein; (bottom row): Audrey Sturm; Rebecca Oprea and Rose Przybylski, as the team prepared to compete in the national women's AAU track and field championships in San Antonio, Texas, on Friday, June 27, 1947. Walsh captured the 200-meter run in pacing her team to a second-place finish. The 39-year-old Clevelander also finished second in the broad jump, losing to Lillie Purifoy of Tuskegee Institute in Alabama, winners of the senior division team championship for the 10th time in 11 years. Tuskegee Institute scored 107 points- 52 more than the Polish Olympic A. C. Missing from the picture were Helen Leick and Peggy Anderson.

(Right) ALEXANDER WINTON, February 17, 1912

The city's annual automobile show opened in Central Armory on Saturday, February 17, 1912, with an elaborate display of 250 autos representing 43 manufacturers. That day, The Press published an interview with Winton Motor Carriage Co. president Alexander Winton (right), builder of the first automobile ever run in Cleveland. "Ultimately, the horse will disappear from our thoroughfares," stated Winton, while smoking a "big black perfecto." "By occupying less space in the street than a team and wagon, the truck will do much towards the elimination of traffic congestion." In 1897, Winton completed the first auto trip from Cleveland to New York. In 1898, he made the first auto sale in the world, selling a one-cylinder vehicle he built for $1,000.

(Left) MAYOR TOM JOHNSON AND HIS WINTON RED DEVIL, Circa 1905

Popular Cleveland Mayor Tom L. Johnson (right at left), who served four terms as the city's chief executive from 1901 to 1911, rests in his trademark Winton Red Devil with son Loftin at the wheel. Johnson's driver sits in the back seat. Behind the men is Johnson's picturesque Millionaire's Row mansion at 2342 Euclid Avenue. During his tenure as the city's top public servant, Johnson established playgrounds, built public bathhouses and popularized public parks. The Mall Plan and Group Plan became reality during his administration. Upon his death in 1911, some leaders referred to Johnson as "the best mayor of the best governed city in the nation."

(Right) WITH JERRY COLONNA, June 13, 1943

"Every 5¢ contributed will buy a package of cigarettes for a serviceman," was one of the selling points used at Municipal Stadium on Sunday, June 13, 1943, as Bob Hope and Jerry Colonna (left center), helped raise money for the Ernie Pyle-Variety Post Overseas Cigarette Campaign. Between games of a doubleheader, Hope directed a group of volunteers, including 75 Fenn College Air Cadets, to fan through the crowd of 13,000 for contributions. After collecting over $1,100, the number of cigarettes headed for our fighting men overseas passed the 9 million mark.

Baseball & Bob Hope

(Above right) AT THE MIKE, June 20, 1948

Hope, a minority owner of the Indians, takes a spell at the WJW Radio microphone to crack a few jokes on Sunday, June 20, 1948, during the Indians game against the Philadelphia Athletics, as team owner Bill Veeck celebrated his second year of owning the team. A record crowd of 82,271 saw the first-place Tribe win both games, 4-3 and 10-0. Next to Hope in the broadcasting booth is WJW's Jimmy Dudley.

(Left) WITH LOU BOUDREAU & JACK BENNY, March 30, 1950

"While the Indians were on the Coast, Lou Boudreau received some expert (?) advice on how to run the Indians from a couple of guys with high batting averages in the comedy league- Bob Hope (left), and Jack Benny," offered The Press on Thursday, March 30, 1950. At the time, Boudreau (center), was concerned about playing starter Bob Lemon in a relief role after using the right-hander in relief to beat the Chicago Cubs in Los Angeles.

Jimmy Hoffa

On Saturday, July 25, 1959, Joann Triscaro, the daughter of local Teamsters Union leader Nunzio Louis (Babe) Triscaro (center, lower left greeting Hoffa), married Sam Busacca at St. Dominic Catholic Church in Shaker Heights. The star attraction that day was national Teamsters Union chief James R. Hoffa (second from right below), who told reporters, "I just came here for Babe's daughter's wedding and to wish her and her husband the best of everything. I'm not here to make controversial statements." Other guests included Ohio Teamsters President William Presser; U. S. Sen. George H. Bender; boxer Rocky Marciano; Port Director William J. Rogers, the only local public official; and "the top echelon of the Cleveland rackets," including Big Al Polizzi, John Scalish and Milton Rockman. That evening, after hosting 250 dinner guests in a mezzanine ballroom at Hotel Carter, a reception was held for more than 1,500 in the hotel's Rainbow Room. The mezzanine ballroom was turned into a dance floor for guests dancing to the music of Marty Conn's Orchestra.

at the Triscaro-Busacca Wedding, July 25, 1959

Some Infamous...

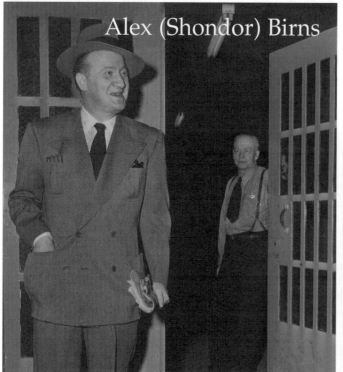

Alex (Shondor) Birns

(Left) LEAVING COUNTY JAIL, January 21, 1950

On Saturday, January 21, 1950, one day shy of seven months since he began serving a sentence for assaulting a policeman, local crime boss Alex (Shondor) Birns walked out of County Jail under a $60,000 bond. The jovial Birns, wearing the same suit he entered jail with in June, was in the midst of being re-tried for allegedly joining four others in masterminding a bomb plot to shake down Hoodlum Joe Allen and extort his numbers racket.

(Right) GETTING A BITE TO EAT, October 7, 1952

After being fed several days of cold sandwiches in the East Cleveland jail, Birns, serving 15 days for driving with a suspended license, left his cell on Thursday, October 7, 1952, for a noontime lunch at nearby Delmar Restaurant, 14306 Euclid Avenue. After his meal, Lieut. Albert Yahraus ran back to jail with Birns.

Sam Sheppard (No. 13 lower right at left), as a member of the 1940-41 Cleveland Heights High School basketball squad.

(Below) WITH ARIANE & CHIP, 1964

"The young Sheppard appears shy. But he speaks firmly when he says that he's convinced of his father's innocence," wrote Press reporter Norman Mlachak on Thursday, August 6, 1964, after 17-year-old Sam Sheppard, Jr. (below left), was reunited with his father (right). The reunion took place after Sheppard, who had spent nearly ten years behind bars at the Ohio Penitentiary, had his conviction for murdering his wife set aside by a Federal District Court judge. With the Sheppard men is Sam Jr.'s stepmother Ariane TebbenJohanns. Sam Jr., who reportedly called Ariane "mother" or "mom," served as an intermediary carrying messages between his incarcerated father and the Dusseldorf divorcee while his father was in jail.

(Below right) WITH F. LEE BAILEY, November 16, 1966

Sheppard attorney F. Lee Bailey (left), joins Ariane and Sam during a press conference at Hollenden House after the Bay Village osteopath was found not guilty on Wednesday, November 16, 1966.

(Bottom left) THE DIVORCE, 1968

Ariane appears before reporters after announcing her desire to seek a divorce from Dr. Sam Sheppard on Tuesday, December 3, 1968.

(Bottom right) AS A PRO WRESTLER, 1969

"I've got some nostalgic but regurgitating memories of this city. But I guess any mistakes the people of Cleveland have made they've already apologized for," Dr. Sam told a reporter after making his local professional wrestling debut before 5,000 at Cleveland Arena on Thursday, October 2, 1969. Sheppard teamed with veteran grappler George Strickland, at right taping Sheppard's ankle, to beat Jack Murphy and Mike Lorin. In the main event, Bobo Brazil and Great Igor teamed to beat The Sheik and "Wild Bull" Curry. Sheppard, who claimed he was broke, said he learned to wrestle in the state pen.

Dr. Samuel H. Sheppard

At Municipal Stadium
During the Ninth Annual National
Scholastic Band Contest
May 16, 1936

The 9th Annual National Scholastic Band Contest, 1936

More than 18,000 spectators gathered in Municipal Stadium on Saturday, May 16, 1936, to watch over 7,000 students from 26 states participate in the day-long Ninth Annual National Scholastic Band Contest. In one of the most dramatic sweeps ever registered by a city in the biennial music battle, three local schools, John Adams, Cleveland Heights and Shaw High captured Division 1 ratings in the Class A competition, establishing Cleveland as the scholastic music center of the United States. In addition, Lakewood High won

Division 1 honors in the marching competition. As the event came to a close, drummers were called to encircle the field on the cinder track, while drum majors formed a star in the middle of the field. From the bleachers, 5,000 student musicians from 72 massed bands performed a final musical salute with renditions of "Stars and Stripes Forever," and "Semper Fidelis," producing a sound that shook the stadium and reverberated through parts of downtown. Each band sat one member to a row, forming a rainbow-like quilt of colors. The patriotic finale concluded with the Ohio National Guard lowering the American flag as the musicians played the national anthem.

(Above) Rhodes High band members practice at Municipal Stadium during the National Scholastic Band Contest.

(Left) Members of the Lakewood High Band, one of the top honor winners in the marching competition, practice in front of Public Hall during the Ninth Annual National Scholastic Band Contest. In the background is the city's old Central Armory.

On Monday, December 3, 1951, The Press reported, "Ring out the bells. Start searching for the Yule log. The Christmas season is officially here in Cleveland. It arrived yesterday as the biggest and merriest of The Press Christmas Parades, seen by one of the largest parade

THE CATHEDRAL LATIN BAND,

crowds in history, wound its way through the packed downtown streets." Joining the merry marchers, colorful floats, balloons and of course, Santa Claus, during the annual holiday kickoff were talented area high school marching bands from West, John Hay, John Adams, St. Edward, Central, Glenville and John Marshall. Another outstanding group of scholastic musicians providing "Christmas music and cheery tunes" was the Cathedral Latin High Marching Band at left, under the direction of John Hruby.

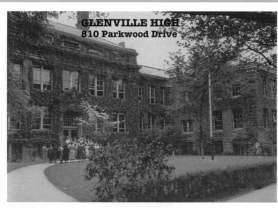

GLENVILLE HIGH
810 Parkwood Drive

EAST TECH HIGH
E. 55th and Scovill Ave.

Going to High School in 1933

On Monday, May 22 and Tuesday, May 23, 1933, The Press highlighted 4,500 graduating seniors from local and suburban high schools. The paper also included photographs of the schools producing the soon-to-be graduates awaiting "those coveted sheepskins."

SOUTH HIGH
3901 E. 74th St.

LINCOLN HIGH
3001 Scranton Rd.

WEST TECH HIGH
2201 W. 93rd St.

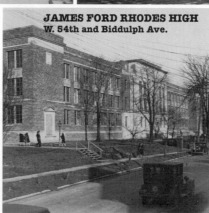

JAMES FORD RHODES HIGH
W. 54th and Biddulph Ave.

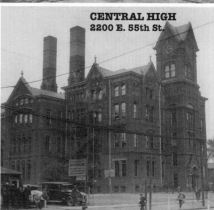

CENTRAL HIGH
2200 E. 55th St.

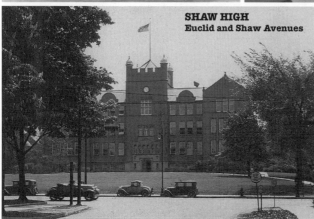

SHAW HIGH
Euclid and Shaw Avenues

JOHN HAY HIGH
2075 E. 107th St.

(Right)
COLLINWOOD HIGH,
October 22, 1929

The drinking of bootleg "hooch" in area schools was under investigation by School Board officials on Tuesday, October 22, 1929, when Press reporter James P. Kirby wrote, "At Collinwood High School (right), where principal Frank P. Whitney said that bootleg drinking was a serious problem last year, the complaint is that during a rehearsal of one of the school's three orchestras, a flask had been passed around among the boys by one of the orchestra members." Whitney told Kirby, "There were numerous instances last year when teachers, in return for favors the boys sought, were offered liquor the boys said came from their father's cellars."

(Right) CELEBRATING
NATIONAL EDUCATION WEEK,
AT JOHN ADAMS HIGH,
May 19, 1938

To help celebrate National Education week in 1938, open houses were held during school hours at schools throughout the Cleveland system. Some schools offered special demonstrations during the open houses, including John Adams High, at 3817 E. 116th St., where the gymnasium captains at right were scheduled to take part in a physical education demonstration at 3 P.M. on Thursday, May 19, 1938.

(Right) THE FOOD BUYING
CLASS AT SHAW HIGH,
November 21, 1941

Amber brand hams were 55¢ a pound at the new Euclid-105th market, "the shopping center of the east side;" ground meat was 25¢ a pound at Fisher's Master Markets, and Clock brand bread sold for 19¢ a loaf at local Kroger stores on Friday, November 21, 1941, when The Press reported on Shaw High students receiving "a practical education in retail buying from a course taught by R. P. Louis." The newspaper stated, "Students learned to know when foods live up to the labels and what the labels should say. Samples of well known brands are tested for various essentials of good food." In the class at right were George Jewett of 13506 Graham Road (left); Walter Williams of 14304 Euclid Avenue; Patricia Gallagher of 14620 Terrace Road; Jack Lewis of 14109 Ardenall Road; Helen Bell of 145005 Alder Avenue and Ruth Franzen of 9921 Foster Avenue (right).

(Left)
TYPING CLASS AT WEST HIGH, February 3, 1932

On Wednesday, February 3, 1932, The Press reported, "West High School today took over the crown of pupil congestion laid down by South High, which entered a new building Monday." At the time, 2,500 students were schooled in the building built for only 1,050. "There is little prospect for immediate relief," West High principal David P. Simpson told The Press. "Lake Avenue is building up with apartment houses, bringing a tremendous increase in students. We have 100 more than a year ago. Every 45 minutes, the building thunders and shakes as 2,500 students crowd through hallways." At left, 75 pupils were squeezed into a typing class in one of West High's basement classrooms were only 48 typewriters were available. Basement corridors were used as a makeshift lunchroom.

Dedicating Benedictine High School
November 16, 1941

An estimated 5,000 men, women and children of Slovak ancestry celebrated the dedication of Benedictine High School at 2900 East Boulevard, S. E., on Sunday, November 16, 1941. Auxiliary Bishop James A. McFadden blessed and dedicated the $375,000 building, a culmination of 14 years of work of the Benedictines in Cleveland. Afterward, Rev. Fr. John T. Humensky, pastor of St. Anthony-St. Bridget's Catholic Church, served as master of ceremonies over the speaking program which included remarks by Mayor Frank J. Lausche; Mrs. Mary Lorenc of the First Catholic Slovak Ladies' Union; John Sabol of the first Catholic Slovak Union, Jednota; Rt. Rev. Msgr. John R. Hagan, superintendent of schools in the Cleveland Catholic Diocese; the Rt. Rev. Msgr. Francis J. Dubosh and Stanislaus Gmuca, head of the Benedictine Abbey in Cleveland. Mayor Lausche offered that while destruction was rampant in the rest of the world, "it was a great solace to know that more schools and churches were being built in this country." The program ended with a dedicatory banquet in the school gymnasium. The school originally opened in September of 1940, but a boiler explosion on November 1, 1940 caused $30,000 damage to the structure, delaying dedication ceremonies until the following year.

(Upper left) The dedication program began with a parade from East Blvd. and Kinsman Rd. to the school.

(Left) Bishop James A. McFadden participates in the dedication ceremonies. Built to house 850 students, 460 pupils attended classes when the school was dedicated.

(Right) THE BOILER EXPLOSION, November 1, 1940

The damage was estimated to be around $30,000 after a boiler exploded in newly opened Benedictine High School on Friday, November 1, 1940. The explosion, blamed on a faulty steam valve, blew chunks of 2 1/2" reinforced concrete flooring through the roof, but because it was a Catholic holy day, no students were in the building. On a normal day, over 125 students would have been in a heavily-damaged study hall area above the boiler room.

(Right) **LEARNING RETAIL AT JOHN HAY HIGH,** April 23, 1940

When The Press published the photograph at right on Monday, April 23, 1940, the paper reported, "Here is one of the reasons why John Hay High School, E. 107th street and Carnegie avenue, holds its ranking as the most outstanding school of

its kind in the country." Diana Greenberg (right at left), demonstrates "the store technique which is taught in the school," to senior classmates Filomena Di Francesco (left), Margaret Moore, Elizabeth Lesiak, Valerie Augustine, Elfrieda Rudnicki and Jean Kilgore (right). Most of the students held part-time jobs in local retail stores.

(Right) **FUND RAISING AT ST. IGNATIUS HIGH,** April 21, 1966

Charging a dime a try, or three swings for a quarter, St. Ignatius High students raised $48.50 towards their annual scholarship fund on Thursday, April 21, 1966, by allowing students to smash used cars with 15-pound sledge

hammers in the school parking lot. Over 350 students took part, as freshman and sophomore students belted away on the 1954 Mercury sedan, while junior and senior classes demolished a nearby 1957 Ford station wagon. A local junk yard donated the two cars.

GLENVILLE HIGH WELCOMES DR. MARTIN LUTHER KING, JR.

"Books, not bricks will win the Negro's fight for full civil rights," Dr. Martin Luther King, Jr. (at podium), told the 3,500 students assembled at Glenville High on Wednesday, April 26, 1967. The famous civil rights leader was in town for a series of meetings culminating in a major talk that night at Olivet Institutional

April 26, 1967

Baptist Church. King also told the assembly, "If you are a street sweeper, sweep the streets the way Michelangelo painted. Be the best of whatever you are." King also spoke to students at Addison Junior High and East Tech High. During his stay, King remarked to students, "Cleveland can be the first major city of have a black mayor."

Pursuing Higher Education in Cleveland

(Above)

Raising Funds, Wednesday, October 10, 1923

John Carroll University Girls Motor Corps members Agatha Millmore (left), and Ella Dobscha (right), display posters used to promote their school's $3,00,000 foundation campaign. The Motor Corps, under Millmore's leadership, was responsible for distributing literature to the 21 local parish chairmen assisting their fund raising efforts. Several thousand women from Catholic societies also assisted in the foundation appeal.

CLASSES BEGIN AT FENN COLLEGE, September, 1931

(Right) As Fenn College students prepared for the start of fall classes on Monday, September 15, 1931, the incoming freshman in line at right were waiting for their initiation, which included a friendly whack of the paddle.

(Below) Fellow students look on as upperclassman Raymond Kamp (with paddle), prepared to "welcome" freshman Robert Heck.

At Fenn College FENN

(Cleveland State University)

(Below) AT THE SCHOOL'S NEW CAFETERIA, June 14, 1943

Mrs. Alice J. Lewis served freshman Marjorie Strauss (below left), and pre-junior Paul Leonard of the student war council, from the soda fountain in Fenn College's new cafeteria on Monday, June 14, 1943.

(Above right) NEW CO-ED ENGINEERS, October 29, 1953

On Thursday, October 29, 1953, Press reporter Jack Warfel wrote, "A record crop of coeds was reported heading for the monkey wrenches today at Fenn College's School of Engineering." Warfel attributed the rise to a shortage of trained, available male engineers for non-military posts. Above right, Margaret Stevens (left), and Rita Martin took ultra high frequency measurements on a slotted line under the guidance of Prof. William C. Davis in Fenn College's electrical laboratory.

(Right) CELEBRATING THE END OF FINALS, August 29, 1959

Fenn College students closed E. 24th St. from Chester to Euclid Avenue on Friday, August 29, 1959, for a "Spring Summer Fling," in celebration of the end of final exams. Jerry Simon's band supplied the music for over 1,000 students, faculty members and gate crashers who took part in the six-hour fun fest. A midway was established in one of the parking lots.

(Left) COMMENCEMENT EXERCISES, June 14, 1937

Baldwin-Wallace College's 87th annual commencement took place on Monday, June 14, 1937, with seniors forming at Wheeler Hall (at left), before marching to Fanny Nast Gamble Auditorium where Dr. George E. Carrothers of the University of Michigan delivered the commencement address. Miss Margaret Blosser, Miss Lillian McLean, Miss Clara Buehl, Miss Amy Brown and Miss Wilma Riemenschneider graduated magna cum lauda in the class of 87 seniors.

(Below) IN THE CLASSROOM, May 19, 1959

Baldwin-Wallace assistant professor William Allman works with Sue Turner (left), during a freshman speech class. Press reporter Bud Weidenthal wrote on Tuesday May 19, 1959, "Prof. Bill Allman is a 35-year-old bundle of energy. The professor runs, he says, because he likes it. Likes teaching that is- despite his $4,700 annual salary."

(Right) PLAYING FOOTBALL, July 25, 1944

Baldwin-Wallace head football coach Ray Watts addresses line candidates Bill Smith, Gene Balcom, Gene Degyansky, Bill Burns and Julius Tonges as fall practice began on Monday, July 25, 1944. Though most of the 52 candidates possessed little experience, among returning veterans were FB Lee Tressel, HB Jim Roberts, tackles Bill Burns and Jack Bevan, E Tom Skillman and QB Hank Benedict.

Baldwin-Wallace College

(Below) ZETA THE LION, August 26, 1957

Sitting majestically in front of the Baldwin-Wallace fraternity house Sigma Phi Epsilon at 72 Bagley Road, Zeta the Lion received its annual fall cleanup from frat brothers Jess Petty, 21 (left), and Jim Mayley, 20. Dousing Zeta with coats of paint was such a favorite trick of student pranksters that house president Al Roesch told The Press for a story on Monday, August 26, 1957, "After two days of freshman week, she'll have a rainbow colored hide."

(Below) MAY DAY CHARIOT RACE, May 10, 1947

The men of Lamda Chi Alpha fraternity receive the winners trophy from college publication queen Dorothy Frick after capturing the annual chariot race during the school's May Day activities on Saturday, May 10, 1947. Five men rode in the wagon, while five others provided the muscle power, navigating their wooden "chariot" along a 440-yard course on Seminary Street in downtown Berea.

(Above) BREAKING GROUND, April 7, 1931

A steam shovel provided the backdrop when Bishop Joseph Schrembs turned the first sod for John Carroll University's new $2.5 million home at Miramar and Belvoir boulevards in University Heights on Tuesday, April 7, 1931. With Schrembs were Msgr. Joseph F. Smith of St. John Cathedral (left); Rev. Albert C. Fox, S. J.; Rev. Benedict J. Rodman, S. J.; Chesapeake & Ohio president John J. Bernet and Herman R. Neff (right). Classes were scheduled to be moved to the new quarters from the school's home on W. 30th near Lorain Avenue in early 1932. The university's fund raising campaign was led by a $110,000 donation, the campaign's largest single gift, from the children of Caesar A. Grasselli. **(Above right)** John Carroll University's new main campus under construction on Monday, December 12, 1931. When completed, the first phase was expected to accommodate 1,500 students.

(Right) GRADUATION DAY, June 2, 1942

With Americans immersed in war, "America must either reintegrate in Christ or disintegrate," Rev. John E. Readon, S. J., of New York told the 164 graduating seniors at right on Tuesday, June 2, 1942, during the combined commencement exercises of John Carroll University, Notre Dame College and Ursuline College held on the John Carroll campus.

John Carroll University

(Above) THE GRASSELLI BELLS, October 24, 1935

"John Carroll Students Hail The Press Candid Camera," offered The Press on Thursday, October 24, 1935, above a series of photographs taken at the university. One image featured the student above with the Grasselli Bells housed in Grasselli Tower.

(Right) CHEMISTRY CLASS, January 31, 1949

"Laboratories of chemistry, biology, and physics departments at Carroll contain gleaming bewildering arrays of the newest equipment," wrote Press reporter Jack Warfel on Monday, January 31, 1949, for a story on the junior class at John Carroll, who paid "from $40 to $80 a semester for rooms, about $210 a term for board." "Card playing is not permitted in the dormitories. For relaxation, students play board games, listen to radios or enjoy programs on one of Carroll's college-constructed TV sets in the recreation room." According to Carroll registrar Eugene R. Mittenger, the junior class of 1949 represented the last class made up predominantly of military veterans.

Case Tech

(Left) GRADUATION DAY, April 11, 1930

The school was celebrating its 50th year of existence on Friday, April 11, 1930, when Case president Dr. W. E. Wickenden led graduates from the Administration Building of Case School of Applied Sciences to John Hay High, where commencement exercises were held. Dr. Wickenden was officially installed as the school's new president during the morning ceremony. Under construction behind the student brigade is Severance Hall.

(Below left) GOING TO THE MOVIES, October 22, 1938

Case students take a break from the books by taking in the weekend matinee at Keith's 105th theater at E. 105th Street and Euclid Avenue on Saturday, October 22, 1938.

ON THE CAMPAIGN TRAIL,
                                    April 23, 1952

On Wednesday, April 23, 1952, Press reporter Jack Warfel wrote, "Case Tech today began its greatest political campaign (a Republican one), sparked by a campus operating fund of $1,500." On Friday, April 25th, Republican presidential candidate Harold Stassen addressed delegates at Severance Hall. On Wednesday, April 30th, the group's two-day convention opened with a two-hour parade that evening featuring eight queens including Miss Donna Howard (below, center). A dance in Tomlinson Hall followed the parade. On May 1st, prominent Oklahoma Republican William Alexander spoke to the delegates with Republican gubernatorial candidate Charles P. Taft serving as Parliamentarian.

(Above) THE UNDERCLASS BAG FIGHT, Oct. 16, 1948

After Case underclassmen held their annual bag rush at New York Central field on Saturday, October 16, 1948, the contestants above, "minus some clothing but covered in mud and grease," marched down Euclid Avenue to E. 105th St., "generally upsetting things," by blocking cars and pulling trolleys off wires. As 100 victorious freshman were marching in a body to "wash up" in Wade Park lagoon, a team of twenty mounted police and foot patrolmen arrived to disperse the students. One freshman was arrested and charged with disorderly conduct.

Graduation Day, 1932

Over 1,100 Western Reserve University students and their families attended the first graduation exercises held at Severance Hall on Wednesday, June 15, 1932. The convocation address was delivered by W. R. U. President Robert E. Vinson who warned, "The world will view you as an added embarrassment- just so many more looking for work that does not exist." But he also added, "larger tasks than ever awaited the truly educated person." Vinson conferred honorary doctor of law degrees on Dudley S. Blossom and Dr. Lafayette B. Mendel of Yale University. The university abandoned its traditional single commencement at Adelbert Gymnasium in 1932, allowing its 13 schools and colleges to conduct separate exercises after the convocation at buildings throughout University Circle. Ohio Supreme Court judge Florence Allen spoke to Flora Stone Mather grads at the Church of the Covenant.

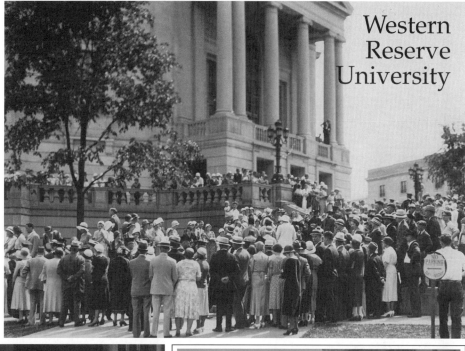

Western Reserve University

(Right) Francis F. Prentiss (left), Dr. Charles F. Thwing, Dr. James D. Williamson and John L. Severance at Severance Hall on June, 15, 1932.

PROTESTING FOR PEACE, April 12, 1935

On Friday, April 12, 1935, nearly 3,000 Western Reserve University students rallied in the school's gymnasium against war and voted on resolutions linking the school with other educational institutions in a common move to outlaw warfare. **(Above)** Following the peace rally, more than 1,000 marchers, half the group coeds, took to the heavily-traveled streets around University Circle chanting, "We want no more war."

(Below) GREEK WEEK, April 20, 1966

"One more reassuring sign of spring," is how The Press described the Greek Week banners strung by the school's fraternities and sororities across Bellflower Rd. near Ford Dr. on Wednesday, April 20, 1966.

(Above) GRADUATION DAY, June 14, 1950

The longest commencement march at the time in Western Reserve University history took place on Wednesday, June 14, 1950, when 1,213 graduates participated in commencement exercises. Above, the winding procession reaches the halfway point as Flora Stone Mather girls head into Severance Hall where University president Dr. John S. Mills addressed the all-university morning assembly. Among recipients of honorary degrees was George M. Humphrey, president of M. A. Hanna Co.

(Right) ALVA BRADLEY WITH E. S. BARNARD, November 28, 1927

New Tribe president Alva Bradley (left), meets with former Indians president and new American League president Ernest S. Barnard (right), shortly after buying the team in November of 1927 from the estate of the late Big Jim Dunn for a reported $950,000. On Monday, November 28, 1927, Bradley announced during a dinner at the Tavern Club, that major league umpire and sports writer Billy Evans had been hired as the club's first general manager, making Evans the first GM in American League history. Among the managers being suggested to Bradley were Tris Speaker, Roger Peckinpaugh, Casey Stengel and Ty Cobb.

(Below) BILL VEECK, July, 1946

New Tribe president Bill Veeck, Jr. (left), meets with Leo Conway to discuss plans for the upcoming Amateur Day program at the Stadium on Sunday, July 14, 1946. 18,000 attended the annual event, raising $1,000 for the Cleveland Baseball Federation.

(Below) VERNON STOUFFER, March 17, 1970

Graig Nettles' play at third base was called a pleasant surprise during spring training in Tucson, Arizona, when manager Alvin Dark (left), GM Gabe Paul and owner Vernon Stouffer, held a meeting of the minds at Hi Corbett Field. Two days after a story about the three men appeared in The Press on Tuesday, March 17, 1970, flamboyant outfielder Ken (The Hawk) Harrelson broke his right leg, complicating their decision making.

Baseball in Cleveland
The Owners

(Right) NICK MILETI, April 1, 1972

When new Indians owner Nick Mileti appeared in The Press on Saturday, April 1, 1972, with the bumper sticker at right, rookie manager Ken Aspromonte's squad had voted 27-0 the night before to support a strike called by the Major League Baseball Player's Association.

CLEVELAND
Del Unser cf
Eddie Leon 2b
Alex Johnson lf
Graig Nettles 3b
Chris Chambliss 1b
Ray Fosse c
Buddy Bell rf
Frank Duffy ss
Gaylord Perry p
MILWAUKEE
Rick Auerbach ss
Dave May cf
John Briggs 1b
George Scott 3b
Joe Lahoud lf
Bill Voss rf
Paul Ratliff c
Ron Theobald 2b
Bill Parsons p

"Well...It's a real world, baby," said Mileti. "Everybody does what he feels he has to do. Right now I'm trying to define our role in the ball club in meetings with Gabe Paul. I had planned to meet with the team, but that's impossible under the circumstances." Mileti was in New Orleans with the Indians who were scheduled to play an exhibition game with the Chicago Cubs. Mileti was also meeting with officials of the city's Superdome about the possibility of playing games in the new domed stadium.

(Right) Starter Gaylord Perry gives new owner Nick Mileti tips on throwing a baseball before the Cleveland Indians' Opening Day game on Saturday, April 15, 1972. The Indians lost, 5-1, to the Milwaukee Brewers before 22,831 at the Stadium as Perry, who gave up nine hits, took the loss. The Indians finished the year in fifth place with a 72-84 record, 14 games behind the pennant-winning Detroit Tigers.

Baseball-
The Early Days

(Right)
THE U. S. BASEBALL LEAGUE CLEVELAND FOREST CITYS, May, 1912

The Cleveland Forest Citys, at right, of the short-lived United States Baseball League, played their first game at the city's old Luna Park Stadium before only 3,696 on Wednesday, May 1, 1912, losing to Pittsburgh, 11-7. Though Reading and Richmond, the two small city clubs drew well, league teams in New York, Chicago, Cincinnati, Pittsburgh and Washington were no match for their major league counterparts. After only three weeks of play, the Cleveland club folded. (top row): C. Hobart, Rafferty, Kirby, Britten, Stringer, Selig, Wakefield; (middle): Freeman, Ort, Pfeifer, O'Connor (manager), Walters, Miller; (bottom): Shaylor, M. Hobart, Green, Delahanty, Blancke.

The First Major League Baseball Game at Municipal Stadium

July 31, 1932

On July 30, 1932, the third-place Cleveland Indians lost to the second-place Philadelphia Athletics, 7-2, before 5,000 at League Park. The following day, the Indians played their first home game away from E. 66th and Lexington Ave. in 41 years, moving to Municipal Stadium where they faced the A's in a Sunday contest before 80,184, major league baseball's largest crowd at the time. That morning, 38,000 tickets went on sale at Municipal Stadium- 17,000 unreserved

(Above) Formal ceremonies began at 1:30 P.M., with the introduction of veteran Cleveland baseball stars including Tris Speaker (left), Napoleon (Nap) Lajoie and Chief Zimmer (right), who paraded around the stadium and then helped local Marines raise the American flag.

grandstand seats at $1.10; 11,000 unreserved pavilion seats (covered) at 85¢; and 10,000 bleacher seats at 55¢. The festivities began at 12:30 P.M., with Jimmy Johnston's 60-piece orchestra leading an informal parade to the Stadium. The league-leading A's beat Cleveland, 1-0, as Robert Moses (Lefty) Grove, who gave up four hits, outdueled young Indians starter Mel Harder, who hurled a six-hitter. Both men pitched shutout ball until the eighth inning, when Philadelphia scored the only run.

Walter 'Big Train' Johnson-
The Tribe's New Manager
June 9, 1933

On Friday, June 9, 1933, Cleveland Indians president Alva Bradley issued the following statement: It is with great disappointment that the board of directors of the Cleveland Baseball Co. finds it necessary to change managers at this time. For five years every effort has been made to build a winning team in Cleveland. Roger Peckinpaugh has worked hard and done everything in his power to make a winner. He is a Cleveland boy and it is unfortunate at this time to make this change. We have given very careful thought to his successor and have decided to employ Walter Johnson as manager. His experience

both as a player and manager should be most helpful. Walter Johnson will arrive in Cleveland Saturday, but will not take charge of the team until Sunday, June 11th. The game Saturday, June 10, will be in charge of Bib Falk, coach."

(Above) Johnson (second from right above), was greeted upon his arrival at Union Depot on Saturday, June 10, 1932, by a large party of local dignitaries including Mayor Ray T. Miller, seen shaking hands with Johnson. Second from left is Indians president Alva Bradley. At right is Indians GM Billy Evans.

(Left) Johnson, who was signed through the 1934 season, addresses his new team before making his managerial debut on Sunday, June 11, 1933. The Indians made Johnson's start a success, beating the St. Louis Browns, 1-0, before 8,000 at the Stadium, as reliever Oral Hildebrand got the win. Johnson compiled a 179-168 record with the Indians before being replaced by Indians coach Steve O'Neill in 1935.

STARTING LINEUPS
CLEVELAND
Lyn Lary ss
Bruce Campbell rf
Odell (Bad News) Hale 2b
Jeff Heath lf
Earl Averill cf
Hal Trosky 1b
Ken Keltner 3b
Rollie Hemsley c
Bob Feller p

NEW YORK
Frank Crosetti ss
Red Rolfe 3b
Tommy Henrich rf
Joe Di Maggio cf
Lou Gehrig 1b
Bill Dickey c
Jake Powell lf
Bill Knickerbocker 2b
Monte Pearson p

JOE DI MAGGIO IS HONORED,
May 22, 1938

On Sunday, May 22, 1938, the Cleveland Indians beat the second-place New York Yankees, 8-3, before 62,244, the largest crowd of the season, at Municipal Stadium. Prior to the game, Yankee slugger Joe DiMaggio (third from right), was honored with watches and a floral wreath by members of the Italio-American Nation Union. Standing with the Bronx Bomber are Rickey Ianno (left), president of the local chapter, Yankee teammate Frank Crosetti, Bill Ianni and Thad Fusco. Center fielder Earl Averill starred for the Tribe, driving in four runs with two singles, while DiMaggio went hitless in four trips to the plate. Mel Harder got the win in relief. During the game, Yankees ironman Lou Gehrig left with a pulled muscle in his back, but returned the next day to start his 1,993rd consecutive contest.

"FARGO RAY" MACK ARRIVES, August 8, 1938

Former local sandlot and Case School of Applied Science star Ray (Mack) Mlckovsky (left at right), joined Tribe manager Oscar Vitt (far right), at League Park on Thursday, September 8, 1938, after his contract had been purchased from the Springfield team of the Mid-Atlantic League. Called "200 pounds of man among athletes," by Press columnist Ben Williamson, Mack was leading the Northern League in hitting for the Fargo-Moorehead team, when he got the call to come home. Upon arriving, he received a uniform from the 1935 season. The local lad, "who changed his name to Mack for box score purposes," broke into the big leagues the next day, playing two innings at second base with another young hopeful, Louis Boudreau, at third base. Both men went hitless, as second-place Cleveland lost to the Detroit Tigers, 11-5.

After receiving a leave of absence from the Cleveland Indians, 18-year-old class president Robert William Andrew Feller picked up his high school diploma from Van Meter Consolidated School in Van Meter Iowa, where "the two roads that cross aren't even paved," on Friday, May 14, 1937. The event was carried by radio to the nation over the National Broadcasting Co.'s blue network. Following the ceremony, the young right-hander and his parents traveled by train to Chicago where the second-place Indians were playing the White Sox. Rejoining the squad in Chicago on Saturday, May 15th, Feller (left), was welcomed back by Tribe manager Steve O'Neill (right).

Bob Feller, the Early Days

(Right) **WITH CY YOUNG, May 8, 1941**

The Press offered on Friday, May 9, 1941, "Standout pitchers of two generations exchanged pleasantries in the Indians' dugout when Cy Young, Cleveland's Hall-of Famer, discussed pitching technique with Bob Feller, No. 1 moundsman of today. Rapid Robert appears to be well pleased to get the immortal Cy's advice." Young (left with ball), joined 12,000 at League Park who watched the second-place New York Yankees beat the league-leading Tribe, 5-4. Red Ruffing, who homered, got the win over Al Smith.

1942

1943

Lou Boudreau

THE SEASON BEGINS
April 14, 1942

When the Indians opened the 1942 season against the Detroit Tigers in Detroit on Tuesday, April 14, 1942, making his debut as Tribe skipper was player-manager Lou Boudreau, at age 24, the youngest manager in major league history. Starter Jim Bagby got the win as Boudreau's teammates made his debut a success, beating the Tigers, 5-2. Boudreau went 2 for 3 with a double.

(Above) The 1942 Cleveland Indians.

(Far left) Lou Boudreau (left), chats with his predecessor and new Tribe GM Roger Peckinpaugh before the game.

(Left) **LOU BOUDREAU WITH STEVE O'NEILL, April 21, 1943**

Boudreau met with Detroit Tigers manager Steve O'Neill before Cleveland battled the Tigers in the home opener before 13,647 chilled fans at Municipal Stadium on Wednesday, April 21, 1943. The Indians won, 1-0, as Jim Bagby pitched a brilliant complete game, three-hitter for the win. Bagby also hit a long fly in the ninth inning that drove in right fielder Roy Cullenbine for the winning run.

Al Rosen

(Left) WITH BOB LEMON, August 10, 1951

After hitting four doubles, two singles and a home run in the last four games, Indians third baseman Al Rosen added to his hit production on Friday, August 10, 1951, with a double and a clutch game-winning, two-run homer. Rosen's seventh-inning blast gave starter Bob Lemon (right at left), his 13th win of the year, a 6-4 complete-game victory over the Chicago White Sox before 44,990 at the Stadium. Rosen's 18th homer of the year came off right-handed Chicago starter Hal Holcombe with first baseman Luke Easter on base. During the game, Lemon gave up a home run to former Indian Minnie Minoso, Minoso's first against the Indians.

Lemon's victory was the 56th complete game pitched by Cleveland starters over the season. The win put manager Al Lopez's squad in a first-place tie with the New York Yankees.

(Left) WITH ROCKY COLAVITO, January 11, 1955

In town to help the Indians sell tickets for the upcoming season on Tuesday, January 11, 1955, Rosen (right at left), who had just signed a new contract for "about $38,000," joined 21-year-old rookie outfielder Rocco (Rocky) Colavito in the press room at Municipal Stadium. The 6' 3" Colavito, who had just gotten married, was considered to be the team's "dark horse," according to GM Hank Greenberg after hitting 38 homers at Indianapolis in 1954.

STARTING LINEUPS

CLEVELAND	CHICAGO
Dale Mitchell lf	Nellie Fox 2b
Bobby Avila 2b	Bud Stewart lf
Larry Doby cf	Minnie Minoso 3b
Luke Easter 1b	Eddie Robinson 1b
Al Rosen 3b	Ray Coleman cf
Al Simpson rf	Al Zarilla rf
Ray Boone ss	Bud Sheely c
Jim Hegan c	Chico Carrasquel ss
Bob Lemon p	Hal Holcombe p

(Right) HARDER, SCORE, FELLER, May 1, 1955

Three generations of Indians pitching, pitching coach Mel Harder (left), rookie southpaw Herb Score and ace right-hander Bob Feller (right), gathered around the microphone after contributing to 1st-place Cleveland's doubleheader win over the Boston Red Sox on Sunday, May 1, 1955. Feller beat Boston in the first game before 26,595, 2-0, with his 12th career one-hitter, holding a no-hitter until the seventh inning. Score beat the Red Sox in the second contest, 2-1, on a four-hitter, striking out 16, including the first nine batters. Score's success was credited in large part to Harder, who changed Score's grip on his curve ball. The three All-Stars combined to pitch 7,966 innings for the Indians over 23 seasons, with 4,483 strikeouts and 538 victories in 1,267 games.

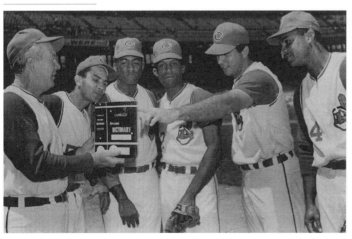

(Left) BIRDIE TEBBETS, June 22, 1965

Cleveland Indians manager Birdie Tebbets (far left), holds up a Spanish-English dictionary to his five Spanish-speaking ball players on Tuesday, June 22, 1965. Tebbets was reportedly learning Spanish to communicate with outfielder Vic Davalillo from Venezuela, pitcher Luis Tiant from Mexico; Chico Salmon from Panama, catcher Joe Azcue from Cuba and Pedro Gonzales from the Dominican Republic.

(Right) CY BUYNAK #1/2, July 4, 1971

It was "Family Day" at Municipal Stadium on Sunday, July 4, 1971, as 11,264 watched the fifth-place Indians take on the last-place Washington Senators. During the day, an informal softball game, umpired by Senators first baseman Frank Howard, pitted Indians players against their wives. At right, pint-sized Indians equipment manager Cy Buynak pleads during the game with umpire Howard. The Indians lost their second-straight to the Senators, 9-4, as starter Steve Dunning, who gave up a homer to Howard, took the loss.

(Far left) CY YOUNG, April 23, 1913

The Press reported on Thursday, April 24, 1913, "Cy Young, signed up late Wednesday as manager of the Cleveland Federal League team, is busy lining up local amateurs and professionals in and around Cleveland for tryouts for the team." At left, Young signed his contract to manage Cleveland's new Federal League entry on the 23rd with Mr. Bramley, the team owner. Practice was set to begin at Luna Park on the 25th with the season slated to start on May 10th. The Cleveland Feds finished the year in second place behind Indianapolis, winning 63 games under Young's guidance, but folded before the 1914 season began.

(Left) EARL AVERILL, March 2, 1934

Tribe manager Walter Johnson looked on as star outfielder Earl Averill (right above left), opened his 1934 contract on Thursday, March 2, 1934. After looking at the number presented by General Manager Billy Evans, who cut some 30% from his 1933 salary of $14,500, the power hitter stomped out of the office to play pinochle. Averill joined Wesley Ferrell, Glenn Myatt and Willis Hudlin among the holdouts as the Indians headed for spring training camp in New Orleans, Louisiana that night. He later signed a deal calling for $10,000 and $300 a homer if he hit more than 30 that season. Averill hit 31 homers in 1934.

Signing Contracts

(Below) LOU BOUDREAU, January 25, 1949

As cameras recorded the action, Indians owner Bill Veeck burned Tribe player-manager Lou Boudreau's old contract on Tuesday, January 25, 1949, after Boudreau, who led the Indians to the World Series championship, signed a new two-year deal worth a reported $65,000 a year.

BOB FELLER'S NEW CONTRACT, January 21, 1948

"It's as good as any contract I ever signed with the Indians," right-handed ace Bob Feller told Press reporter Frank Gibbons on Wednesday, January 21, 1948, after agreeing to a one-year deal estimated to be around $80,000 with attendance bonuses. Above, Feller (left), joked with team owner Bill Veeck after signing his 10th Tribe contract. Veeck remarked, "Bob still has a chance to remain the highest paid player in baseball. He's still better than anyone in the league and he's getting paid for it."

(Left) ROCKY COLAVITO, January 20, 1959

Before being honored as Indians' Man of the Year during the annual Ribs & Roast banquet at Hotel Hollenden on Monday, January 20, 1959, popular right-fielder Rocky Colavito (left), signed his 1959 contract with Tribe GM Frank Lane (right). Colavito's contract was worth a reported $29,000, almost double his 1958 salary, after hitting .303 with 41 HRs, 148 hits and 113 RBI. That night, Tribe manager Joe Gordon predicted, "Rocky Colavito soon will be baseball's greatest star and its biggest fan attraction. Not in the distant future but the next season." Colavito batted .257 in 1959, with 42 HRs, 151 hits and 111 RBI.

"Open season for autograph hunters is any day the Cleveland Indians are playing at the Stadium," wrote Press reporter Bill Dvorak on Wednesday, May 20, 1949, in a feature story about how fans fought for autographs from the American League champs after their daytime match with the New York Yankees on May 19th. **(Upper Right)** Center fielder Larry Doby makes a mad dash from fans while Tribe pitcher Early Wynn **(Far Right)**, stops for nearly 20 minutes to pacify the young "pencil wielders." "Fleet-footed Larry Doby generally depends on his speed to escape," Dvorak offered. **(Right)** Catcher Jim Hegan leaves Municipal Stadium with young son Mike as "teen-agers, bobby-soxers and blue-jeaned gals," followed the Tribe catcher. Player-manager Lou Boudreau was the only Indians player permitted to park inside the ballpark. 11-year-old Raymond Royak told Dvorak he was gunning for Lemon, Bearden, Hegan and Paige. "I'll hang those names in my bedroom," the young autograph seeker exclaimed.

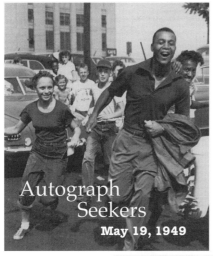

Autograph Seekers
May 19, 1949

Signing Autographs

(Left) PICTURE DAY, May 28, 1967

Though he didn't play in the fourth-place Indians' 5-0 loss to the New York Yankees on Sunday, May 28, 1967, Tribe right fielder Rocky Colavito was a very popular player on "Picture Day." Approaching the Tribe star at left is little J. Jay Smith of Frewsburg, NY. During the Yanks' victory, Yankee veteran Mickey Mantle belted his 507th homer.

(Above) WITH LEN BARKER, August 4, 1981

With the baseball player's strike over, the Indians returned to the Stadium for a light workout on Tuesday, August 4, 1981. During the workout, the young fans above sought the autograph of celebrated Tribe starter Len Barker, who had pitched a perfect game at the Stadium on Friday, May 15, 1981. Barker was one of two Tribe pitchers (with Bert Blyleven), set to play in baseball's strike-delayed All-Star game at the Stadium on Sunday, August 9, 1981.

The price was reported to top $1.5 million when 32-year-old ex-Marine Bill Veeck, Jr. (right at left), completed the purchase of the Cleveland Indians major league baseball franchise from a syndicate headed by Alva Bradley (left at left), on Saturday, June 22, 1946. "The Indians were sold today, lock, stock and League Park," wrote Press reporter Frank Gibbons. Among the new stockholders were comedian Bob Hope and Harry Grabiner, former Chicago White Sox vice president and general manager.

(Lower left) Cleveland Baseball Co. directors I. F. Frieberger, Bradley, William Bernet, John Sherwin, Jr., King White (standing), Francis Sherwin and Joseph C. Hostetler, attorney for the ball club and the American League, met to ratify the sale of the Indians to Veeck at the Union Commerce Bank Building. Missing from the meeting were Morris

The Bill Veeck, Jr. Era (1946-1949)

A. Bradley and Elton Hoyt II. Hostetler became the only director from the old regime retained by Veeck. Of the seven wealthy Clevelanders who purchased the franchise from the estate of Bill Dunn in 1927- Bradley and his older brother Charles, Hostetler, O. P. and M. A. Van Sweringen, John Sherwin, Sr. and Newton D. Baker, only Bradley and Hostetler were alive to see the team sold. The sale included two minor league teams, League Park and all players under contract, including the club's premiere asset, ace pitcher Bob Feller.

(Below left) Player-manager Lou Boudreau and Bob Feller (right), joined Veeck as he attended his first game as new Indians owner, a doubleheader loss to the Boston Red Sox on Sunday, June 23rd before 52,720 at Municipal Stadium. "He's a go-getter, this guy Veeck," wrote Press reporter Henry Andrews. "He jumps all over the park at every game, sitting in from 10 to 15 different seats, listening, asking for, or seeking information as to how to make baseball in Cleveland a better show." "We aren't going to hold any pig races," Veeck told patrons, "But it isn't going to be dull, bet on that."

(Above right) WITH DIZZY DEAN, April 23, 1947

During the Indians' 5-0 win over the St. Louis Browns before 3,629 at the Stadium on Tuesday, April 23, 1947, Veeck joined colorful sportscaster Dizzy Dean (above right) in the broadcast booth. Ace right-hander Bob Feller pitched a one-hitter for the win, facing only 29 batters. Dean told his audience, "Mr. Robert Speedball Feller is throwing so hard down there it's makin' Ol' Dis' arm hurt." Dean was making his first appearance in Cleveland since 1936 when Feller, "then a pink-cheeked rookie," struck out eight of Dizzy's St. Louis Cardinal teammates during three innings of a League Park exhibition match. Press reporter Bob Yonkers wrote in his story on Dean, "Diz says he can't understand why Veeck wants to install a fence in the Stadium. "They're always making it tough on us pitchers and givin' those big bruisers a break.""

(Left) RETURNING HOME, October 8, 1948

Veeck is mobbed by fans after returning home from Boston during the World Series on Friday, October 8, 1948.

(Right) LADIES' DAY AT LEAGUE PARK, July 3, 1946

One of first moves Bill Veeck (center), made as new owner of the Indians, was returning Ladies' Day games to the team's home schedule. The first Ladies' Day matinee in five years was held at League Park on Wednesday, July 3, 1946, as the Indians, with Bob Feller on the mound, played the St. Louis Browns. "Glad to meet you. I hope you see a good game and that you'll be back again for the next Ladies' Day," Veeck told the women at right, who were the first in line to pay 35¢ plus tax for their seats as the gates opened at 10:30 A.M.

(Below right) NOVEMBER 11, 1946

Before leaving for Los Angeles to attend baseball's winter meetings in November of 1946, Veeck reported, "We aren't going to give anybody away, but you can say that we are still hot to do business." **(Below right)** Among the Indians rumored to be trade bait were Ken Keltner, Les Fleming, Ray Mack and George Case, when Veeck, who had just been released from Cleveland Clinic after having part of his leg amputated, met with business manager Rudie Schaffer (left), player-manager Lou Boudreau and Harold (Spud) Goldstein to discuss strategy on Tuesday, November 11, 1946.

(Above) Bill Veeck meets with part-owner Bob Hope and New York Yankees president Del Webb during the Indians' first night game of the year at Municipal Stadium on Friday, May 23, 1947. Cleveland lost to the St. Louis Browns, 5-3, before 61,227, who were entertained by Hope and a midget race before the game.

(Right) JOE EARLEY NIGHT, September 28, 1948

A yellow 1949 Ford convertible with red upholstery, a television set, a radio, a refrigerator, a new dishwasher, a horse described as "only a medical check-up away from a baseball cover factory," a cow, a calf, seven pigs, a goat, some chickens, and a lifetime pass to any American League baseball park, were among the gifts bestowed on Joe Earley and his wife June, by Bill Veeck during 'Good Old Joe Earley' Night at Municipal Stadium on Tuesday, September 28, 1948. The 24-year-old war veteran received his special night after winning a "Mr. Average Baseball Fan" letter writing contest sponsored by The Press. Veeck also gave away live turkeys, 100-pound cakes of ice, step ladders, white rabbits, guinea pigs and bushels of fruit to the crowd of 60,405, and presented orchids, flown in from Hawaii at a cost of $30,000, to the first 20,000 women entering the stadium. Tribe starter Gene Bearden pitched a four-hitter, beating the Chicago White Sox, 11-0.

1948- A World Series Season

(Left) STARTING THE SEASON, March, 1948

After finishing the 1947 season in fourth place, player-manager Lou Boudreau's Cleveland Indians opened spring training camp in Tucson, Arizona on Saturday, February 28, 1948. Providing the cornerstone to Cleveland's defensive threat were Ken Keltner at third base (left), Boudreau at shortstop, Joe Gordon at second base and Eddie Robinson at first base. On July 13, 1948, Keltner, Gordon and Boudreau all started for the American League in the annual All-Star game.

(Right) SECURING A TIE, October 2, 1948

The Cleveland Indians clinched a tie with the Boston Red Sox for the American League pennant by

beating the Detroit Tigers, 8-0, on Saturday, September 2, 1948 before 58,238 at Municipal Stadium. Getting the win for Cleveland was 6' 4" rookie southpaw Gene Bearden (above), who recorded his 19th win and 6th shutout of the season.

(Right) CLINCHING THE PENNANT, Oct. 4, 1948

After losing to the Detroit Tigers in the last game of the regular season, the Indians finished in a dead heat for first place with the Boston Red Sox. The deciding game was played at Boston's Fenway Park on Monday, October 4, 1948. Led by a 13-hit attack, including two homers by shortstop Lou Boudreau and one by third baseman Ken Keltner, the Indians clinched Cleveland's first American League pennant since 1920 at 3:54 P.M., beating the Red Sox, 8-3. Starter Gene Bearden pitched a complete game, three-hitter.

(Far right) Bearden is carried off the field by his jubilant teammates.
(Right) Boston manager Joe McCarthy congratulates Boudreau, who went 4 for 4, after the Tribe's victory.

On Wednesday, July 7, 1948, Negro League hurler Leroy (Satchel) Paige (below left), showed his "stuff" at the Stadium to team owner Bill Veeck (with crutches), and manager Lou Boudreau. His performance impressed Veeck enough to sign Paige that day. Paige later recounted that he threw 50 pitches and missed the corner only a couple of times. "I troubled Mr. Lou and got signed." When he made his debut in an Indians uniform, the ageless hurler became the first black to pitch in the American League. Paige appeared in 21 games during the 1948 regular season, winning six out of the seven games he started (.857), including back-to-back shutouts, with one save and a 2.47 ERA. Paige also appeared once in a relief role during the 1948 World Series. When Paige joined the Tribe roster, Cleveland became the second major league team with two blacks in uniform. (Jackie Robinson and Roy Campanella played for the NL Brooklyn Dodgers.)

Satchel Paige

(Left) WITH HARRISON DILLARD, September 8, 1948

After winning Olympic gold by capturing the 100-meter dash at the London Olympic Games, local track star Harrison Dillard was honored by the Indians on "Harrison Dillard Night" at Municipal Stadium on Wednesday, September 8, 1948. Above, Harrison is joined in the Indians dugout by Paige, who appeared briefly in the game, striking out a batter in relief. Third-place Cleveland beat the Detroit Tigers, 8-7, in 11 innings before 43,707, as reliever Sam Zoldak got the win.

(Right) "Shrewd street vendors, armed with victory pennants, were stationed every 100 feet along Euclid. They had no problem unloading the pennants in jig time," offered The Press on October 5th. The Press also stated that area bars were packed, doing brisk business until closing time.

The City Celebrates

October 4, 1948

"There was a college atmosphere to the downtown celebration," exclaimed The Press on Tuesday, October 5, 1948, after Cleveland beat the Boston Red Sox to capture the American League title on October 4th. "Auto horns blared, snake dances were formed and fireworks exploded. As the evening wore on, high school-age youths seized whatever opportunities they could to kiss girls that passed them. Some of the girls didn't seem to mind. Others did and whacked the too enthusiastic young men soundly." **(Below)** Upon their return home by train on Tuesday, October 12, 1948, player-manager Lou Boudreau (left) and team owner Bill Veeck hopped into the convertible below joining teammates in a World Series victory parade from Terminal Tower.

(Right) Dorothy Sadens (left), and Therese Mackiewicz model pennant aprons made by Nona Lou, Inc. at 632 St. Clair Ave. The company received over 50 dozen orders, including one for the waitresses in Higbee's Silver Grill. The wives of Indians players also received one as a gift.

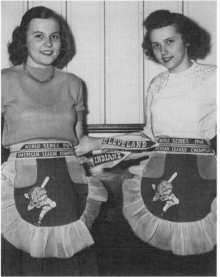

The Tribe's Pennant Parade

September 21, 1954

After the Indians clinched the American League pennant in Detroit on September 18, 1954, the city honored its baseball warriors with an 18-mile motorcade throughout the city on Tuesday, September 21, 1954. "Cleveland did itself proud with a tremendous turnout and a thundering ovation for the Cleveland Indians in yesterday's Pennant Parade, and the players loved every minute of the East-West Side auto procession,"

offered The Press on Wednesday, September 22, 1954. The newspaper reported the biggest crowds were found at E. 105th-Euclid Avenue, Euclid Avenue at Public Square and Kamm's Corners.

(Above) Fans lined the street to greet their heroes as the parade turned from West Blvd. onto Lorain Ave. **(Left)** Fans cheer on the Tribe caravan as it passed Shaw High School. Police estimated over 300,000, including "a trillion school children," cheered on the procession as it traveled across the city from Ivanhoe Rd. to Kamm's Corner.

Spring Training

(Left) SPRING TRAINING BEGINS, February 18, 1927

"Here is the first picture of Cleveland's baseball hopes taking in the sun at Hot Springs, Ark.," offered The Press on Wednesday, February 18, 1927, after Cleveland players and their wives began arriving for spring training. The paper added, "Pitchers George Uhle and Joe Shaute, also are absentees. They preferred to do their early conditioning on handball courts in Cleveland, but when they see this picture it's a safe bet they wished they were in Arkansas. And how do you like the Redskins' nifty new sport jackets." Basking in the daytime light were southpaw Walter Miller (far left), right-hander Willis Hudlin, catcher Chick Autry, right-hander Ollie Perry, right-hander Emil Levson, southpaw Carl Powell, new manager Jack McAllister, coach Harry Matthews, catcher Glenn Myatt and Mrs. Myatt.

(Left) CARL HUBBELL & WALTER JOHNSON, Wednesday, April 4, 1934

"Two of the boys who know something about throwing a baseball," is how The Press described New York Giants starter Carl Hubbell (left), and Indians manager Walter Johnson, who were caught chatting before a spring training game in Montgomery, Alabama on Wednesday, April 4, 1934. Frankie Pytlak and Joe Vosmik led the charge, with Mel Harder getting the win, as Cleveland beat Hubbell and the Giants, 7-0.

(Right) ROY & MIKE, APRIL 5, 1938

Outfielder Roy Weatherly, the shortest Indian at 5 feet, 6 inches, chatted with 6-foot, 8-inch pitcher Mike Naymick, the tallest player on the Tribe roster, before the Indians battled the New York Giants at Texas A. and M. College in College Station, Texas on Wednesday, April 5, 1938. Cleveland beat the Giants, 6-3, as Earl Whitehill got the win.

(Left) LARRY DOBY & JOE DI MAGGIO, March 10, 1951

Coming off a fourth-place finish in 1950, six games behind the New York Yankees, the Indians began spring training in 1951 at Tucson, Arizona, with a new manager, Al Lopez, and one of baseball's top pitching staffs led by Early Wynn, Bob Lemon, Mike Garcia and Bob Feller. On Saturday, March 10, 1951, the Indians played their exhibition opener at Hi Corbett Field, beating the Yankees, 6-5, in a 12-inning contest. Only a week before the opener, veteran Yankee center fielder Joe DiMaggio (right at left), announced that 1951 may be his last season. Joining DiMaggio on the 10th was Indians center fielder Larry Doby, who was coming off a stellar year in which be batted .326 with 25 home runs. DiMaggio retired at the end of the season, succeeded in 1952 by future Hall-of Famer Mickey Mantle. Doby finished 1951 with a 20 home runs, 132 hits and a .295 average.

COLAVITO, MARIS & WOODLING, 1958

New manager Bobby Bragan's Cleveland Indians started spring training in March of 1958 at Tucson, Arizona with outfielders Rocky Colavito (left), Roger Maris and Gene Woodling (right), vying for starting positions. Only Colavito played the entire season for GM Frank 'Trader' Lane, who traded Woodling to the Baltimore Orioles and Maris to the Kansas City Athletics. Rocky batted .303 for the Indians in 1958 with 113 RBI and a team-leading 41 home runs.

(Above) SPRING TRAINING, 1954

Tribe hurlers Mike Garcia (left), and Bob Feller joined third baseman Al Rosen (right), for a Bev Rich break at Hi Corbett Field as spring training began in March of 1954. Rosen won the American League MVP title in 1953 with 43 home runs, 145 RBI and a .336 average.

(Left) THE STARTING LINEUP, 1960

Chugging along with manager Joe Gordon during spring training were the men expected to start the season for the Indians at Municipal Stadium on Wednesday, April 20, 1960. Behind Gordon are Jimmy Piersall, Bubba Phillips, Johnny Temple, Rocky Colavito, Tito Francona, Vic Power, Woody Held, Russ Nixon and right-hander Gary Bell.

(Left) SAM MCDOWELL, February 24, 1964

Rookie Tribe southpaw Sam McDowell (left), one of the early arrivals to spring training camp at Tucson, Arizona, loosens up under the supervision of coach Elmer Valo. McDowell was expected to duel with fellow rookie southpaw Tommy John for a starting slot, but like John, reported to camp with a sore shoulder. "So what had shaped up as a battle of two young left-handers for a starting role on the club has now become a medical experiment which will be watched closely by the Tribe," wrote Press reporter Regis McAuley on Monday, February, 24, 1964.

(Right) BIRDIE'S POW-WOW, February 27, 1965

Tribe manager Birdie Tebbetts holds his first "pow-pow" of spring training in Tucson, Arizona on Friday, February 26, 1965, with Tribe players pitcher Ralph Terry (left), third baseman Max Alvis, right fielder Chuck Hinton, 2nd baseman Dick Howser and left fielder Leon Wagner (right).

League Park
at E. 66th & Lexington

(Left) JOHNNY KILBANE VS. DANNY FRUSH, September 17, 1921

The feature match of the five-bout boxing card at Dunn Field (League Park) on Saturday, September 17, 1921, pitted 32-year-old native-son Johnny Kilbane (right in the ring), in defense of his featherweight title, against Englishman Danny Frush, a journeyman fighter hailing from Baltimore. An estimated 20,000 fight fans "from all over the country," saw what was described as "one of the most spectacular battles ever staged in Cleveland." Knocking the challenger down with powerful rights in the third and fifth rounds, Kilbane, the cagey veteran, finished Frush with a vicious right at one minute, 24 seconds into the seventh round of the 12-round battle. Kilbane took home $60,000 for the win, while Frush received $2,500 for the drubbing.

When the world-champion New York Yankees arrived on Monday, July 11, 1927 for a four-game series with the Indians, The Press offered, "It's bad enough for an American League pitcher to have to face Babe Ruth (right), but when Lou Gehrig (left), and Tony Lazzeri follow right behind, the pitcher is entitled to all your sympathy. The Babe has knocked in 29 home runs so far this year and Gehrig is tied with him. Both Babe and Lou are six behind the schedule Babe was on in 1921, when he set a record with 59 for the season." Urban Shocker pitched the Yankees to victory on July 12th, beating the sixth-place Indians, 7-0, before 6,000 at Dunn Field. Southpaw Joe Shaute took the loss, giving up a home run to Ruth who was greeted at the plate by Gehrig. Press Sports Editor Stuart Bell wrote the next day, "The lethargic Indians got six runners as far as second base Tuesday, and two of them got as far as third but that was as close as the Tribe came to scoring on the Yankees who wound up their first game of their second visit here with a home run flourish by Babe Ruth." Another paper reported, "Twelve times Babe had been up to the plate socking the ball safely. Come the thirteenth time. Joe Shaute, Indians southpaw, threw a low one. Ruth swung and golfed it over the right field wall and set an altitude record for the season at Dunn Field. "Foul," yelled Umpire Van Graflan. Disgustedly, Babe returned to the plate, rubbed his hands in the dirt, picked up his bat and faced the left-hander again. There came a wide one. "Ball." "Put it over," yelled the fans. "Let him hit it." Don't know whether Joe wished to please the fans or just failed to bend the ball where he wanted to. But Babe never had a better home run ball pitched to him in his life. It was right in his groove and with most of his power in his effort, he swung and drove

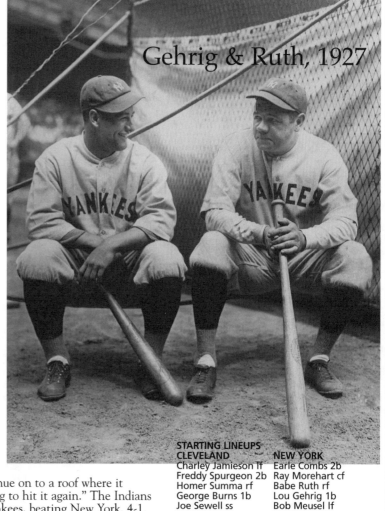

Gehrig & Ruth, 1927

the ball over the wall and screen, over Lexington Avenue on to a roof where it mounded around frantically as if fearing Babe was going to hit it again." The Indians captured one of the four games from the first-place Yankees, beating New York, 4-1, on Thursday, July 14th. Walter Miller, who fanned Gehrig with the bases loaded, got the win. Ruth finished the year with a major league record 60 home runs.

STARTING LINEUPS	
CLEVELAND	**NEW YORK**
Charley Jamieson lf	Earle Combs 2b
Freddy Spurgeon 2b	Ray Morehart cf
Homer Summa rf	Babe Ruth rf
George Burns 1b	Lou Gehrig 1b
Joe Sewell ss	Bob Meusel lf
Luke Sewell c	Tony Lazzeri ss
Ike Eichrodt cf	Joe Dugan 3b
Rube Lutzke 3b	Johnny Grawbowski c
Joe Shaute p	Urban Shocker p

Ladies' Day
at League Park

(Left) CLEVELAND 5, NEW YORK 3, June 4, 1937

The New York Yankees, led by future hall-of-famers Lou Gehrig and Joe DiMaggio, provided the opposition for the second-place Indians on Friday, June 4, 1937, before a Ladies' Day crowd of 13,000 at League Park. Cleveland beat the Yankees, 5-3, as Tribe center fielder Earl Averill went 3 for 4 with a single, double and his fourth home run, while first baseman Hal Trosky rapped two hits, one a triple. The crowd at left roared its approval after Tribe starter Johnny Allen held the Bronx Bombers to one run in the ninth for his third straight win. Allen ended the year with a 15-1 record.

(Right) CLEVELAND 6, ST. LOUIS 0, July 3, 1946

One of the first moves new Tribe owner Bill Veeck, Jr. promised he would make after purchasing the club in June of 1946, was to resurrect popular Ladies' Day matinees at Indians home games. Under Veeck's guidance, the first Ladies' Day game in five years took place at League Park on Wednesday, July 3, 1946, as the Indians battled the St. Louis Browns. The Press reported the line for tickets began forming at 10:30 A.M. "The first woman to nudge past the E. 66th and Linwood box office was Mrs. Mattie Plank, who was greeted by Veeck before entering the park," offered The Press. "In the next 15 minutes another 10 women swarmed around the gate and Veeck was still there shaking hands. They were all unanimous in their reasons for arriving early. They wanted to get the best seats and they wanted to see Bob Feller pitch against the St. Louis Browns." 8,562 paying customers joined 3,397 "screeching gals," in watching Feller lead the fifth-place Indians to a 6-0 win over the seventh-place Browns. It was Feller's 14th win and sixth by shutout, raising his scoreless inning streak to 19. Feller fanned 10, boosting his strike out total to 184 for the season.

The Speed Meter

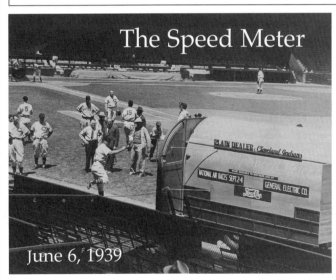

June 6, 1939

special electric beams five feet apart marked the speed of the ball which was then flashed on the machine. After the speed demonstration, the fourth-place Indians rallied before the crowd of 2,000 with a run in the ninth inning to beat the second-place Red Sox, 8-7, as reliever Bill Zuber got the win. A long fly by first baseman Oscar Grimes scored Ben Chapman for the winning run.

(Left) Speed meter inventor John Crawford hands $50 to Red Sox players Roger Cramer (left), Jimmy Foxx and Jim Tabor, the three top throwers, who reached 122 feet per second, or 85 miles an hour. Tribe ace Bob Feller, who threw twice, reached 116 feet per second with his second throw. Boston's five-man squad of Cramer, Tabor, Foxx, Finney and Williams beat Cleveland's five-man squad of Webb, Chapman, Solters, Shilling and Keltner.

"Science can cure your ills, accurately gauge your intellect and make life more understandable all around, but it hasn't reached the point where it can tell you whether your son can become a major league baseball star," wrote Press sports reporter Frank Gibbons on Wednesday, June 7, 1939, after the Indians conducted a "Speed Meter" test before their League Park contest with the Boston Red Sox on Tuesday, June 6th. As players from both teams threw balls into a special trailer,

Professional Football-
The Early Years in Cleveland

1927
THE NATIONAL FOOTBALL LEAGUE CLEVELAND BULLDOGS

1927 RECORD 8-4-1

7	Green Bay Packers	12
0	NEW YORK GIANTS	0
7	New York Yankees (@ Detroit)	13
6	New York Giants	0
12	Chicago Bears	14
21	DULUTH ESKIMOS	20
15	NEW YORK YANKEES	0
0	Frankford Yellow Jackets	22
37	FRANKFORD YELLOW JACKETS	0
22	Providence Steamrollers	0
30	New York Yankees	19
32	Chicago Cardinals	7
20	DULUTH ESKIMOS	0

After supporting National Football League teams from 1920 to 1925, Cleveland's pro football franchise moved to the rival American Football League for the 1926 season. On Tuesday, July 12, 1927, The Press reported, "Cleveland will be represented in the National Professional Football League this fall. Sammy Deutsch, vice president of the newly-formed club, announced Tuesday. Herb Brandt, who with Peggy Parratt backed the local eleven in 1925, is president. Brandt bought the team from Deutsch that year after Cleveland had won the world title in 1924. Deutsch and Brandt will leave for Milwaukee Friday to attend a league meeting at which the season's schedule will be drafted." At the league meeting, the Cleveland contingent obtained the services of former Glenville High star and University of Michigan All-American quarterback Benny Friedman (above right with ball). The Cleveland Bulldogs under coach Leroy B. Andrew (above center), made their league debut on Sunday, September 25, 1927, losing to the Green Bay Packers, 12-7, in Green Bay. Cleveland opened at home the following week on Sunday, October 2nd, playing the champion New York Giants to a scoreless tie before 3,000 at Luna Park Stadium. The Bulldogs finished in fourth place, with an 8-4-1 record, but did poorly at the box office, forcing the team to move after the season. Led by Friedman, who threw for 12 touchdowns and over 1,700 yards, making him the best passer in NFL history, Cleveland led the league in scoring, outscoring their opponents 141 to 26 in the last five games.

1939
THE NATIONAL FOOTBALL LEAGUE CLEVELAND RAMS

1939 RECORD 5-5-1

21	Chicago Bears	30
12	Brooklyn Dodgers	23
27	Green Bay Packers	24
21	CHICAGO BEARS	35
7	Detroit Lions	15
24	Chicago Cardinals	0
14	PITTSBURGH PIRATES	14
14	CHICAGO CARDINALS	0
14	DETROIT LIONS	3
6	GREEN BAY PACKERS	7
35	Philadelphia Eagles	13
	(@ Colorado Springs)	

Following the loss of the Cleveland Bulldogs after the 1927 season, Cleveland fielded a National Football League team only once between 1928 and 1937. In 1931, the Cleveland Indians finished in eighth place with a 2-8 record. On January 14, 1937, Cleveland re-entered the pro loop when a syndicate led by Clevelander Homer Marshman received the league's 10th franchise during the NFL winter meetings in New York City. After finishing 1-10-0 in 1937, and 4-7-0 in 1938, the Cleveland Rams entered the 1939 season with a new coach, Earl (Dutch) Clark, and a new offensive threat in 6', 205 lb. University of Mississippi rookie QB-HB Parker (Bullet) Hall. After opening losses to the Chicago Bears and the Brooklyn Dodgers, the Western Division Rams upset the champion Green Bay Packers, 27-24, in Green Bay on Sunday, October 1, 1939. Falling to 1-4 after losses to the Bears and the Detroit Lions, the Rams jelled in the second half, outscoring their opponents 93 to 37 in the last six games. Led by E Jim Benton, FB Johnny Drake, LT Chet Adams, QB Vic Spadaccini and Hall- No. 32 above with Phil Ragazzo (36)- Cleveland beat the Lions before a record home crowd of 25,000, tied the Pittsburgh Pirates, 14-14, twice beat the Chicago Cardinals and beat the Philadelphia Eagles in Colorado Springs, to finish at 5-5-1. Hall led the NFL in passing, smashing the single-season pass completion mark during the Rams' 7-6 home loss to Green Bay on November 26th, when he completed 14 passes for 90 on the year. Hall was named the league's MVP in 1939.

(Left) PRACTICE BEGINS, July 29, 1946

Beginning barely a month before their first contest, an exhibition match with the Brooklyn Dodgers on August 30th in Akron's Rubber Bowl, Paul Brown's Cleveland Browns opened their first training camp at Bowling Green University on Monday, July 29, 1946. On Tuesday, July 30th, Press reporter Bob Yonkers wrote, "Brown has clamped a non-drinking and no-gambling ban on the team. There's a 10 P.M. curfew. The players haven't been forbidden to smoke, but Brown made it clear that he disapproves of the habit during the football season."

(Below) Len Simonetti (left), from Tennessee, Ernie Blandin from Tulane, Lou Groza from Ohio State and Lou Rymkus from Notre Dame (right), watch coach Bob Voigts demonstrated blocking techniques on Jim Daniell from Ohio State.

1946- The Cleveland Browns Begin Play

(Right) Head coach Paul Brown (with cap) goes over a play with Chet Mutryn of Xavier University and Cathedral Latin as coaches Blanton Collier (far left), and Creighton Miller look on with players Bob Steuber from Missouri and Frank Gatski from Marshall (right).

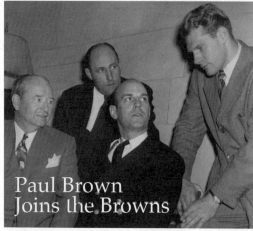

Paul Brown Joins the Browns

COMING ON BOARD, April 17, 1945 "You know me- I'm going to try to build a football dynasty," 36-year-old Lieut. (J. G.) Paul Brown told Press reporter Jack Clowser on Thursday, February 8, 1945, after being picked by Zone Cab Co. owner Arthur B. (Mickey) McBride, to coach and manage McBride's Cleveland franchise in the new All-America Football Conference. **(Left)** Brown (second from right), meets with McBride (far left), and assistant coaches John Brickels and Creighton Miller (right), on Tuesday, April 17, 1945. Brown's five-year deal paid him a reported $25,000 a year plus a percentage of the profits, making him the highest paid coach in pro football. On May 3rd, the Cleveland franchise began a naming contest, offering a $1,000 War Bond to the entry winner. On Thursday, April 12, 1945, Clowser wrote in The Press announcing the contest, "Here are a couple of tips: Don't suggest nicknames that are too lengthy. Long words don't easily fit into newspaper headlines. Also don't suggest that the club be called the Cleveland Browns, just because the former Ohio State coach will be running things. Only about 75,000 other people will think of the same thing and anyway, The Press revealed some weeks ago that Brown plans to follow out a Scarlet and Gray (Ohio State's colors) theme in equiping his team. So, the "Browns" won't do for that reason." On Friday, June 8, 1945, Navy specialist first class John J. Hartnett won the $1,000 bond as one of 35 entries of the over 2,000 submitted, who suggested "Panthers" as the new team's nickname. The next day, former Nebraska tackle Vic Schleich became the first player signed by the "Panthers."

WITH HIS STAFF, March 7, 1946 After returning to civilian life, on Thursday, March 7, 1946, Brown met with staff members backfield coach John Brickels (left), Bill (Red) Conkright, business manager Frosty Frobert, guard coach Fritz Heisler and tackle coach Bob Voigts. Brown's coaching staff grew to five just before training camp with the addition of Blanton Collier. Brown told a reporter, "It is my contention that this can be developed into one of the hottest sports towns in the country. All the fans need is a winner. It is my intention to give them their money's worth for the next five years."

THE BROWNS' FIRST PLANE TRIP, October 11, 1946

On Friday, October 11, 1946, the Cleveland Browns at right, headed to New York to play the New York Yankees in an All-America Football Conference matchup. The plane trip taken by the Browns was the first air departure by a Cleveland team. Upon arriving at New York's La Guardia airport, Browns coach Paul Brown "hearded his unbeaten, untied team to the "House that Ruth Built" for a final pass-defense drill in anticipation of the aerial blitz certain to be launched against them by Fireball Frankie Sinkwich and Orban (Spec) Sanders, the Yankees' ace passers," according to Press reporter Bob Yonkers. The unbeaten Browns raised their record to 6-0 by beating the Yankees, 7-0, at Yankee Stadium on Sunday, October 13th.

(Right)
CLINCHING THE WESTERN TITLE- CLEVELAND 42, BUFFALO 17, November 24, 1946

The smallest crowd of the home season, 37,054, watched the Browns battle the Buffalo Bisons at Municipal Stadium on Sunday, November 24, 1946. Led by the crushing running of FB Marion Motley, who galloped 76 yards for a score and Edgar (Special Delivery) Jones, who scored twice on runs of 46 and 37 yards, the Browns demolished their opposition, 42-17. Also scoring for Cleveland were E Mac Speedie; Al Akins, who rambled 50 yards for the score; Bud Schwenk and Lou "The Toe" Groza, who booted six extra points. With the win, coach Paul Brown's team clinched the Western Division of the All-America Football Conference and cleared the way for an AAFC title match with the New York Yankees on December 22nd.

(Right) Browns E Dante Lavelli (56), smashes through the Buffalo defense for 14 yards with Lin Houston (32), leading the way.

STARTING LINEUP

Player		Position
George Young	(202)	LE
Ernie Blandin	(249)	LT
Ed Ulinski	(200)	LG
Lou Groza	(225)	C
Lin Houston	(205)	RG
Lou Rymkus	(229)	RT
John Yonakar	(218)	RE
Otto Graham	(190)	QB
Edgar Jones	(192)	LH
Ray Terrell	(180)	RH
Marion Motley	(218)	FB

Winning The Browns' First AAFC Title

December 22, 1946

After beating the Buffalo Bisons to clinch the Western Division title on Sunday, November 24, 1946, Cleveland faced the New York Yankees in the first AAFC championship game. Played before 40,469 at the Stadium on Sunday, December 22nd, the Browns beat New York, 14-9, to capture the first of four straight AAFC titles.

(Left) After the game, head coach Paul Brown joined QB Otto Graham (left), who completed 16 of 27 passes, Dante Lavelli, who caught a game-winning pass from Graham with only five minutes to play and E Mac Speedie (right). Brown said after the game, "I wouldn't trade these three boys for any six football players in the world." Each player received a reported $937.00 for winning the championship.

(Left) SKULL SESSION, December 24, 1952

"Defensive and offensive assignments are thoroughly digested then rehearsed each afternoon at League Park," reported The Press on Wednesday, December 24, 1952, after head coach Paul Brown went over the playbook with his players in preparation for their NFL title game against the host Detroit Lions on Sunday, December 28, 1952. Studying their assignments in the front row are guard Abe Gibron (left), tackles Lou 'The Toe' Groza, Jerry Helluin and Bob Gain; quarterback George Ratterman and ends Pete Brewster and Mac Speedie (right).

(Lower left) BUYING THE CLEVELAND BROWNS, July 16, 1953

"Sale of the Cleveland Browns football team was officially completed today when the group of Clevelanders who bought the club from Arthur B. McBride turned over a check for half the purchase price," reported The Press on Thursday, July 16, 1953. The Press further stated, "The group, headed by Dave Jones and Saul Silberman, gave McBride and Dan Sherby a check for $250,000. This added to the $50,000 given earlier as a binder, is half the purchase price agreed upon on June 11th when the sale was announced. The contract was formally signed in the law offices of Homer Marshman, who is also one of the group purchasing the club. Another owner is Ellis Ryan, former president of the Indians." **(Left)** Arthur B. (Mickey) McBride receives the check for $250,000 from new team owner David Jones (seated), on July 16th. Behind the men are Homer Marshman, secretary and general counsel (left), Saul Silberman, chairman of the executive committee, and former VP Edward McBride (right). McBride also received a lifetime pass to all Browns home games "in appreciation of his contribution to football."

(Right) ALONG THE SIDELINE, 1964

On the sideline in December of 1964.

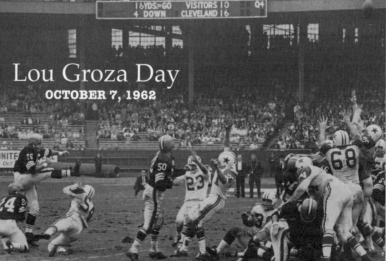

Lou Groza Day
OCTOBER 7, 1962

It was "Lou "The Toe" Groza Day," at Municipal Stadium on Sunday, October 7, 1962, as the Cleveland Browns battled the Dallas Cowboys before 44,040. The Browns evened their record at 2-2 with a 19-10 win over their Eastern Conference challengers, who played both Don Meredith and Eddie LeBaron at quarterback. Cleveland's touchdowns came on a one-yard, first quarter run by FB Jim Brown; and a play put in for the game, "19 rollout." Browns QB Jim Ninowski faked to FB Ernie Green and then passed to Brown, who eluded two tacklers to score on the 50-yard pass play. **(Above right)** Groza kicks the second of two field goals in the fourth quarter, a 42-yarder, that clinched the game for his team. "Nothing would have been the same if we hadn't won the football game. I guess the last field goal felt as good as any I've ever kicked," said Groza, who was honored with his family at halftime. **(Above left)** Groza (right), is joined by family members, brother Alex (left;) Jackie, his wife; his mother; one-year old Judd; Jeff, 9; brother Frank; Jill, 8; and Jon, 7; during the halftime presentation. Among the gifts Groza received were a fire engine red convertible and a color TV. Behind the Groza clan is the Youngstown College marching band.

(Right) SETTING AN NFL RUSHING RECORD, November 24, 1957

"He was terrific, simply terrific," said head coach Paul Brown on Sunday, November 24, 1957, after rookie fullback Jim Brown (32 at right returning a punt), set an NFL rushing record with 237 yards on 31 carries, a 7.64 average, before 65,407 at Municipal Stadium. Cleveland beat the QB Norm Van Brocklin-led Los Angeles Rams, 45-31, as rookie QB Milt Plum, who replaced injured starter Tommy O'Connell, overcame an 11-point deficit for the victory. After the win, Brown, who scored four TDs, one on a 69-yard run, heaped praise on his front line saying, "Give the credit to the blockers. They sure opened holes for me."

No. 32 FB Jim Brown

1957

1958

(Left) SETTING A TEAM RECORD, October 12, 1958

"Blast-em-with Brown and blind-em-with Mitchell," wrote Press reporter Bill Scholl, after a record home-opening crowd of 65,403 watched the Cleveland Browns beat the Chicago Cardinals, 35-28, at Municipal Stadium on Sunday, October 12, 1958. Brown, about to score one of three TDs at left, rushed for 182 yards on 34 carries, a team record. HB Bobby Mitchell (49), making his home debut, carried 11 times for 147 yards. Also in the play were DT Mike McCormack (74), and HB Preston Carpenter (40).

(Right) BROWN'S LAST SCORE, December 5, 1965

Played before a standing-room-only Municipal Stadium crowd of 77,765, the Eastern Conference-champion Cleveland Browns won their tenth game in twelve tries, beating the Washington Redskins, 24-16, on Sunday, December 5, 1965. In the four quarter, Browns FB Jim Brown scored the game-clinching touchdown with less than two minutes left in the game. The touchdown was Brown's 20th of the season, tying the NFL set the year before by Baltimore's Lenny Moore. Brown rushed 27 times for 141 yards, giving the veteran running back the 58th game of 100 yards or more during his nine-year pro career. At right, Brown is greeted after scoring his only TD of the game by Abe Abraham, affectionately known as "the man in the brown suit." It would the last touchdown scored at the Stadium by Brown, who retired before the start of the 1966 season.

1965

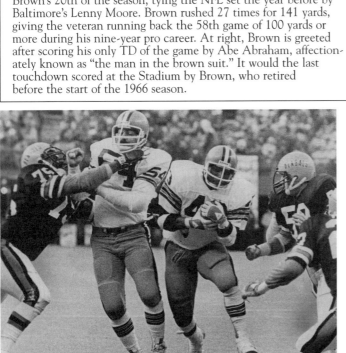

CLINCHING THE DIVISION TITLE / CLEVELAND, 27, CINCINNATI, 24, December 21, 1980

"Scripted in Heaven or Hollywood what other ending would have fit Cleveland's "Kardiac Kids?" The drama, the issue, the Browns' first division championship in nine years, simply had to go down to the final play of the final game of the wildest and whackiest regular season (except there was nothing regular about it) in the 35 years of the franchise," wrote Press sports writer Jim Braham on Monday, December 22, 1980, after coach Sam Rutigliano's Cleveland Browns beat the Cincinnati Bengals, 27-24, before 50,058 at Cincinnati's Riverfront Stadium to clinch the American Conference Central Division title. (Left) Browns center Tom DeLeone leads the way for FB Mike Pruitt, the game's leading rusher, who ran for 16 yards to set up a game-winning, fourth-quarter field goal by 13-year veteran Don Cockroft. Pruitt rushed 14 times for 51 yards, giving him 1,034 for the regular season and his second straight 1,000-yard season. Pruitt also caught 6 passes for 11 yards. Browns QB Brian Sipe completed 24 of 41 for 308 yards and 3 TDs, putting him over 4,000 yards passing for the season.

(Left) PAUL BROWN- THE LAST AAFC CHAMPIONSHIP GAME, December 11, 1949

After beating the Buffalo Bills, 31-21, at Municipal Stadium on December 4, 1949, the Cleveland Browns returned to the Stadium on Sunday, December 11, 1949, to play for the All-America Football Conference championship a record-setting fourth straight year. The game was played against the San Francisco 49ers before only 22,550, partly because of inclement weather and partly because the Browns were playing the 49ers for the third time that season. Cleveland won the title match, 21-7, on scores by HB Edgar "Special Delivery" Jones, who rushed for 63 yards on 16 carries, FB Marion Motley, who ran 67 yards for a TD, and HB Dub Jones on a four-yard plunge. The Browns not only celebrated the AAFC title win that day, but also their move into the new National-American Football League the following year. Because of the low turnout, each Browns player received $226 for the win.

(Left) Browns head coach Paul Brown sits upon the shoulders of HB Edgar Jones after the game as DE George Young (52), and team captain Lou Saban (20), look on. Upper left is Lou "The Toe" Groza, who kicked three extra points in the game.

(Right) BLANTON COLLIER/ NEW YORK 33, CLEVELAND 6, October 27, 1963

"A funny thing happened on the way to the championship. We got muirdered," wrote Press sports reporter Bill Scholl after the Eastern Division-leading Browns lost their first game of the season to the New York Giants, 33-6, before 84,213 at Municipal Stadium on Sunday, October 27, 1963.

(Right) Browns head coach Blanton Collier, in his first year as the team's leader, "looks mighty melancholy," on the Browns sideline while watching his team get manhandled by the quarterback Y. A. Tittle-led Giants. With Collier are Johnny Brewer (left), quarterbacks Frank Ryan and Jim Ninowski and Ross Fichtner.

Coaches &...

(Left) NICK SKORICH, November 15, 1972

"The Bossards report the playing field in excellent shape for Sunday, despite the heavy rains and threats of snow this week," wrote Press sports reporter Bob Sudyk on Wednesday, November 15, 1972, as the Browns prepared to host the Pittsburgh Steelers at the Stadium. At left, Browns head coach Nick Skorich checked in with Stadium groundskeeper Harold Bossard.

(Right) SAM RUTIGLIANO-HEADING TO THE PLAYOFFS, Oct. 26, 1980

Cleveland was preparing for the Carter-Reagan presidential debate at Music Hall the next day, when head coach Sam Rutligliano's Browns beat their Central Division rivals, the Pittsburgh Steelers, before 79,095

at Municipal Stadium on Sunday, October 26, 1980. "Neither wind nor cold nor snow nor the Pittsburgh Steelers nor a storm of mistakes could keep the Browns from their appointed place today in the sun," wrote Press reporter Jim Braham on Monday, the 27th, after Cleveland edged the Steelers, 27-26. Down 26-14 after three quarters, the Browns scored twice in the final quarter on QB Brian Sipe TD passes to HB Greg Pruitt, who made a diving fourth-down catch, and TE Ozzie Newsome, for the victory. Sipe completed 28 of 46 for 349 yards. At right, Browns DE Lyle Alzado (77), hugged Rutigliano after the dramatic win.

(Right) OTTO GRAHAM / WINNING THE NFL CHAMPIONSHIP, Monday, December 26, 1955

"On the second play, the Browns started one of their famous criss-cross, or double cross pass patterns. (Otto) Graham faded far back, awaiting the chance to hit a free receiver. He caught Lavelli unattended on the Rams' 25-yard-line, fed him the ball perfectly and Dante raced over for the score," wrote Press Sports Editor Franklin Lewis after the Browns captured their second straight National Football League crown, beating rookie coach Sid Gillman's Los Angeles Rams, 38-14, before 85,693 at the Rose Bowl on Monday, December 26, 1955. The play Franklin described came after DB Tommy James intercepted a pass from Rams' QB Norm Van Brocklin, one of six picked off by the Browns. Graham, who ended his 10-year career with the win, completed 14 of 25 for 209 yards, passing to Lavelli and Ray Renfro for scores and running for two more, the last score coming on his last rushing attempt as a pro. **(Right)** Graham (14), laterals to HB Ed Modzelewski during the win as OT Mike McCormack (74), looks on. The Browns received a record $3,508.21 per man.

(Right) MILT PLUM / CLEVELAND 28, PITTSBURGH 20, October 2, 1960

The Browns hosted the Pittsburgh Steelers on Sunday, October 2, 1960, before a record home opening crowd of 67,692 at Municipal Stadium. Cleveland won, 28-20, as QB Milt Plum (16), threw for 308 yards to receivers Gern Nagler, Bobby Mitchell and Rich Kreitling. **(Right)** Plum hands off to Mitchell (49), as OG Jim Ray Smith (64), and C Art Hunter (56), lead the blocking.

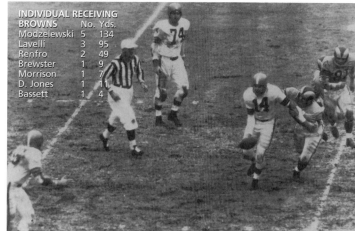

INDIVIDUAL RECEIVING BROWNS	No.	Yds.
Modzelewski	5	134
Lavelli	3	95
Renfro	2	49
Brewster	1	9
Morrison	1	7
D. Jones	1	11
Bassett	1	4

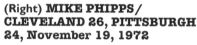

...Quarterbacks

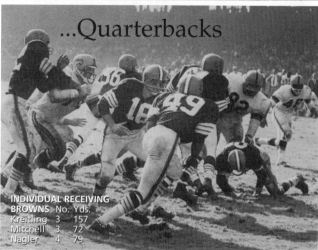

INDIVIDUAL RECEIVING BROWNS	No.	Yds.
Kreitling	3	157
Mitchell	3	72
Nagler	4	79

(Left) FRANK RYAN / October 4, 1964

QB Frank Ryan (13), eludes his pursuit during the Browns' 27-6 win over the Dallas Cowboys before 72,062 at the Stadium on Sunday, October 4, 1964. Ryan completed 15 of 26 for 236 yards with TD passes to Ernie Green, Paul Warfield and third-year pro Gary Collins, who set a team record with TD catches in six straight games.

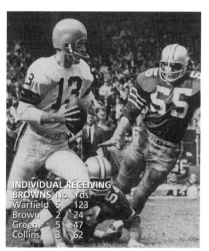

INDIVIDUAL RECEIVING BROWNS	No.	Yds.
Warfield	5	123
Brown	2	24
Green	5	47
Collins	3	62

(Right) MIKE PHIPPS / CLEVELAND 26, PITTSBURGH 24, November 19, 1972

"This was a bigger victory than the last-minute one over San Diego last Monday. It was the biggest one I've ever been in," said Browns QB Mike Phipps after beating the Pittsburgh Steelers, 26-24, before 83,009 at Municipal Stadium on Sunday, November 19, 1972. With only 13 seconds left, Browns place-kicker Don Cockroft booted his second field goal, a 26-yarder, for the win, putting Cleveland in a first-place tie with the Steelers for the Central Division lead. **(Above)** Phipps (15), who completed 15 of 24 for 194 yards, hands off to HB Leroy Kelly (44), with Steelers' DT Mean Joe Greene (75), in pursuit. Kelly picked up his first 100-yard game of the season, rushing 21 times for 107 yards. Phipps ran for one Browns TD and completed a 17-yarder to WR Frank Pitts for the other score.

INDIVIDUAL RECEIVING BROWNS	No.	Yds.
Scott, R.	2	15
Morin	4	77
Pitts	3	43
Kelly	1	10
Hooker	2	25
Glass	2	24

INDIVIDUAL RECEIVING BROWNS	No.	Yds.
Rucker	5	108
Logan	6	87
G. Pruitt	10	75
M. Pruitt	6	42
Newsome	3	28

(Left) BRIAN SIPE / CLEVELAND 17, NEW YORK 14, December 7, 1980

Played before 78,454, the sixth Municipal Stadium sellout in eight home contests, the Browns (9-4), faced the New York Jets (3-11), on Sunday, December 7, 1980. Cleveland won, 17-14, clinching the contest on the five-yard, fourth-quarter TD pass at left from QB Brian Sipe (17), to HB Greg Pruitt (34). Sipe set a team record with 30 completions in 41 attempts for 340 yards, including 10 passes for 75 yards to Greg Pruitt, one reception short of former Browns' receiver Mac Speedie's team record of 11 pass receptions set 28 years earlier. It was Sipe's fifth game of more than 300 yards that season and 10th of his career.

The Browns at Training Camp

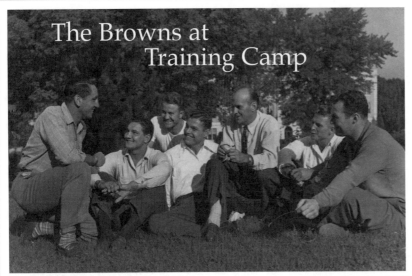

(Left) OSU PLAYERS LEADING THE BROWNS, August, 1946

The Cleveland Browns began their first All-America Football League season in August, 1946 with head coach Paul Brown relying heavily on players he tutored as head coach at Ohio State University from 1941 to 1943. Brown, who led his teams at Massillon High to a 81-7-2 record over 9 seasons before accepting the Ohio State position, led the Buckeyes to an undefeated season, the Big Ten title and the mythical national championship in 1942. One of Brown's first moves after taking over coaching duties with the Browns was to secure the services of former Ohio State players T Lou Groza (left), FB Gene Fekete, G Lin Houston, E Dante Lavelli, G George Cheroke and T Jim Daniell (right). Another OSU standout joining the team in 1946 was G Bill Willis. Brown, Groza, Lavelli and Willis would all later enter Pro Football's Hall of Fame in Canton, Ohio.

(Right) VYING AT HALFBACK, JULY 27, 1948

"The Browns today started banging heads in crisp competition for steady employment and as the first workout got underway it seemed certain that the hottest fights would be waged at the tackle and halfbacks positions," wrote Press reporter Bob Yonkers on Tuesday, July 27, 1948. Among the players competing with former Brooklyn Dodgers starter Dub Jones for a halfback spot were Vince Marotta from Shaker Heights and Mt. Union (left); Bob Brugge from Parma and Ohio State; Ara Parseghian, Miami; Tommy James, Ohio State; Warren Lahr of Western Reserve and Dean Sensanbaugher, Ohio State (right). Yonkers added, "Anyone could crash the starting eleven without causing a great deal of surprise."

(Left) AT QUARTERBACK, July 8, 1959

As the Browns began their pre-season quarterback training camp at Hiram College on Wednesday, July 8, 1959, vying for starting positions were Luthern High and Valparaiso College star George Helms (left); Bob Brodhead of Duke; Hiles Stout of Illinois; Michigan State's Jim Ninowski; former Holy Name and University of Michigan QB Bob Ptacek, who starred in the East-West Shrine Game and Hula Bowl, where he was named most valuable collegian; and Penn State's Milt Plum (right).

(Right) ARRIVING FOR CAMP, July 24, 1961

The Cleveland Browns kicked off the 1961 football season with the opening of training camp at Hiram College on Monday, July 24th. The next day, Press sports reporter Bill Scholl offered, "Paul Brown's lengthy introductory speech, the annual intelligence test, the important all-out 40-yard sprints, the first taste of coaching instructions and an evening meeting set the tone for the next eight weeks." Being counted on heavily as the Browns opened camp were "the younger set of veterans," safety Bobby Franklin (left); end Rich Kreitling; safety Don Fleming; guard Gene Hickerson; halfback Bernie Parrish and tackle Larry Stephens (right).

(Right) BLANTON COLLIER TAKES OVER AS HEAD COACH, July 22, 1963

"We're going to be watched by the entire football world in the coming season and we'll be judged on only one basis- if we win or lose," new Cleveland Browns head coach Blanton Collier (right), told his troops as they began pre-season training at Hiram College on Monday, July 22, 1963. The first year coach added, "Each year you've got to produce, or get out. That's not Collier's law, or Modell's law. It's the law of professional sports."

Leading the returning veterans was FB Jim Brown (above left), with Collier on the first day of camp. After losing the National Football League rushing title to Green Bay's Jim Taylor in 1962, under Collier's new offensive scheme, Brown captured the NFL rushing title for a fourth time in 1963, gaining 1,863 yards on 291 carries. The powerful rusher also scored 12 touchdowns for the Browns who finished at 10-4, good enough for second place behind the Eastern Division-winning New York Giants. In 1964, Collier led Cleveland to the NFL title.

(Above) DICK SCHAFRATH, August 13, 1970

After being informed by head coach Blanton Collier that he was going to see some action in the upcoming exhibition game against San Francisco, Dick Schafrath, above signing autographs at Hiram College on Thursday, August 13, 1970, said, "The arm still aches, but I can live with that." The veteran OT was practicing with a special foam pad protecting his ailing elbow.

(Below) AT TRAINING CAMP, August 2, 1971

New Browns head coach Nick Skorich (far left), addresses his veterans at Hiram College as the team prepared for their exhibition opener against San Francisco.

(Below right) COWHER & MATTHEWS, May 30, 1980

When the Cleveland Browns opened their annual mini-camp at Baldwin-Wallace College on Friday, May 30, 1980, four free agents, safety Billy Cesare, strong safety Steve McCoy, defensive end Glenn Robinson and linebacker Bill Cowher, who had a brief trial with Philadelphia in 1979, joined veteran members of the Browns defense, including Dick Ambrose and Thom Darden, in Berea. **(Below)** Cowher (left), masters his jump rope skills with Clay Matthews. The two linebackers were set to figure prominently in the 3-4 defense of new defensive coordinator Marty Schottenheimer.

(Right) VETERAN'S DAY, May 20, 1972

"Will this be the year Mike Phipps comes into his own as a real-live functioning pro quarterback?" asked Press sports reporter Bill Scholl on Monday, May 22, 1972, after the Browns conducted their veteran's day workout at Fleming

Field on Saturday, May 20th. **(Above)** Participating in the mile run during veteran's day were Browns players Bob McKay, Doug Dieken, Mike Sikich, Gene Hickerson, John DeMarie, Mitch Johnson and Bubba Pena. The top milers were Ernie Kellerman (5:50), Charley Hall (6:06) and Clarence Scott (6:08). Slowest were Gene Hickerson (8:45) and Joe Righetti (9:20). Ken Brown won the agility drill and the 40-yard dash. DE Joe Jones was fastest in the 20-yard dash for linemen.

The Cleveland Arena
on Euclid Avenue

On Monday, September 9, 1968, an investor group headed by Nick J. Mileti completed the purchase of both the Cleveland Barons hockey franchise from Paul Bright and the aging Cleveland Arena on Euclid Avenue. Press sports writer Bob August reported that day, "According to a reliable source, the purchase price of the Barons will be close to $500,000. The price of the Arena is set at approximately $1,250,000. With the addition of legal and accounting fees, the total cost to Mileti's group will approach $2,000,000." August added, "Today's sale will put the Barons and the Arena under the same ownership for the first time since the Al Sutphin era, when hockey enjoyed its greatest popularity in Cleveland. Although the purchasing group has offered no comment on its plans, it is likely that it will make a strong bid for a pro basketball franchise." **(Above)** The Arena at 3715 Euclid Avenue in July of 1942. **(Left)** Barons and Arena owner Nick Mileti, a 1949 John Adams high graduate, stands in front of his sports palace in September of 1970 as his new National Basketball Association franchise, the Cleveland Cavaliers, was preparing to open its inaugural season at the Arena.

(Right) TWO-TON TONY STARTS THE RACE, 1939

Over 4,000 spectators, the largest local crowd to attend a bike race at the time, turned out at the Arena for the first night of Cleveland's eighth six-day bike race on Wednesday, February 1, 1939. Among the special guests that night were Earl (Dutch) Clark, new coach of the NFL Cleveland Rams and boxer "Two-Ton" Tony Galento at right, serving as the race starter. German rider Heinz Vopel, said to be one of the world's best riders, was knocked out after breaking his wrist in a bad five-bike spill.

At the Six-Day Bike Races

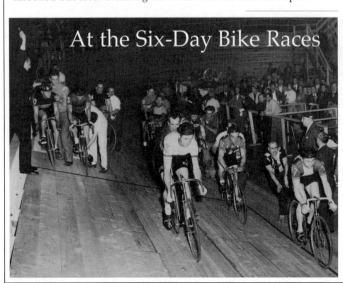

(Left) BOB FELLER STARTS THE RACE, January, 22, 1957

The Arena track was completed only an hour before "the famous right arm" of former Indians ace Bob Feller (far left), fired the starting gun to begin the six-day international bike race on Tuesday, January 22, 1957. Nine nations were represented in the race, the fourteenth held at the Arena and first in seven years. Without sufficient time to practice, eleven riders went down in the first hour. One five-bike crash spilled riders in "Devil's Corner" along the south side of the Arena, sending Italian Nino DeRossi to the hospital with a broken nose. An estimated 3,500 watched the first night of competition as the favored Australian team of Alf Strom and John Tressider captured the lead by a slight margin.

The Arena's Beginning Days

BREAKING GROUND, May 17, 1937

"The shovel, nosing into the soil (far right), erases the imprints of 16 silver shovels which yesterday were wielded by 16 directors of the Cleveland Hockey Club Inc. as they broke ground for the city's new $1,000,000 arena," wrote Press reporter Carl Shatto after ground was broken at 3715 Euclid Avenue for Al Sutphin's palatial Cleveland Arena on Monday, May 17, 1937. The dirt-digging ceremony, which attracted some 500 onlookers, was broadcast over WGAR Radio.

(Above right) Fred Potts (left), secretary of the club, Al Sutphin, Mrs. Helen Braden and Cleveland Falcons coach Harry Holmes (right), four of the club's 16 directors, turn the first dirt at the new project.

(Right) OPENING NIGHT, November 10, 1937

Tickets, available through the Arena ticket office, Bond Clothes at 419 Euclid Ave., or by phone at ENdicott 3700, ranged from 75¢ to $3.30 for the five-day run of "Ice Follies of 1938," the first event hosted at Sutphin's new million-dollar ice palace. The spectacle starring internationally-known skaters Roy Shipstad and Bess Ernhardt opened on Wednesday, November 10, 1937, before a capacity crowd of 8,000, including U. S. Senator Robert J. Bulkley and Mayor Harold H. Burton. Arena management averted a last minute snafu by agreeing to pay fifty union painters $10 for two days to get the building's 9,700 chairs painted.

(Below) EAST TECH HIGH WINS THE CITY TITLE, February 20, 1959

A capacity crowd of 11,402 jammed the Arena on Friday, February 20, 1959, to watch East Senate champs East Tech play St. Ignatius, winners of the West Senate, for the city scholastic basketball title. Led by the play of 6-6 Ken Glenn, the Scarabs beat St. Ignatius, 79-56, to capture the crown and their 43rd straight win. With the win, East Tech became the first team to win the Franklin Lewis Trophy presented annually to the title winner by The Press. In the consolation match, Cathedral Latin's 6-7 junior center Al Payne set an Arena scholastic scoring mark with 33 points, but his Lions were upset by John Marshall, 64-62. Center Len Stafford led Marshall with 16 points.

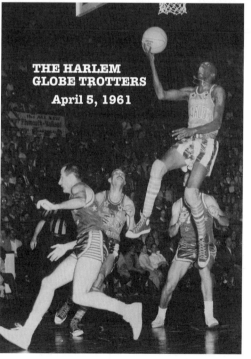

THE HARLEM GLOBE TROTTERS April 5, 1961

Abe Saperstein's talented Harlem Globe Trotters paid one of their many visits to the Arena on Wednesday, April 5, 1961, as a sellout crowd of 11,265 watched the court comedians battle College All-Stars. **(Left)** John Egan watches Meadowlark Lemon leap for the layup during the college cagers' 94-73 loss to the Harlem roundballers. "The crowd loved it enough not to care that the All-Star squad was inferior to those of other years and that the Trotter management didn't bother to report beforehand that Walt Bellamy, the headline collegian, might not appear," wrote Press reporter Ben Flieger. The 6' 11" All-American, nursing an injured heel, did not play.

EAST TECH- 79			ST. IGNATIUS- 56		
Glenn	13	1	27	Gallagher	6	1	13
Porter	5	0	10	Wood	3	0	6
Ferguson	7	0	14	McGinnis	5	3	13
Franklin	3	0	6	Sykora	1	0	2
Stone	5	2	12	Corrigan	3	3	9
Davis	1	0	2	Hegan	6	1	13
Sellers	1	0	2				
Lane	3	0	6				

(Left) THE FIRST SEASON, January 5, 1938

"Cleveland's frost-bitten and hard-bitten ice Barons hitched their hockey wagon to a batch of Eagles (New Haven brand) at the Arena last night and, as a result, have ridden back to within a point of the International-American League lead," wrote Press reporter Carl Shatto on Wednesday, January 5, 1938, after Cleveland's "red, white and blue bruisers" shut out New Haven, 2-0, before 4,992. **(Left)** Eagles goalie Paul Gauthier deflects a shot during the Barons' win, who remained undefeated at home with six wins and three ties at the newly-opened ice palace. It was Barons goalie Moe Robert's second shutout of the season.

Hockey as played by the Cleveland Barons

(Right) THE DEFENDING CHAMPIONS, October 28, 1941

As the defending American Hockey League-champion Cleveland Barons prepared to begin their defense of the title on Tuesday, October 28, 1941, coach Bun Cook announced that his starting lineup would be Moe Roberts in goal, Harry Dick and Capt. Bill MacKenzie at defense, Les Cunningham at center and Joffre Desilets and Norm Locking at the wings. Providing much of coach Cook's offense threat were the team's 11 forwards at right: (front row): rookie Whitey Prokop, right wing; Don Deacon, center; Jake Milford, left wing; (second row): Joffre Desilets, right wing; Les Cunningham, center; Norm Locking, left wing; (back row): Art Giroux, right wing; Earl Bartholome, right wing, left wing, and center; Bud Cook, center; rookie Walter Melnyk, center; and Herb Foster, left wing. On Thursday, October 30, 1941, Press reporter Carl Shatto wrote, "With the American League season only one day old, the local icers already have two records in their credit. 1. They have a full-fledged holdout in Earl Bartholome veteran handy-andy forward from Minneapolis. 2. They attracted 7439 fans, biggest opening game crowd in Cleveland hockey history, to the Arena last night to see them defeat the Pittsburgh Hornets, 6-4."

(Left) CLINCHING THE AHL TITLE, March 6, 1951

After winning the league's "Grand Slam"- the Western Division title, the American Hockey League title and the Calder Cup playoffs- in the 1944-45 and 1947-48 seasons, Barons coach Fred (Bun) Cook was shooting for his third Grand Slam season after his squad clinched the AHL pennant on Tuesday, March 6, 1951. Cleveland beat the Providence Reds, 4-1, before 3,641 at the Arena, winning the title for the sixth time in Cook's eight-year history. At left, Fred Thurier (left), the team's leading scorer, team captain Hy Buller, who scored one of the goals, and Les Douglas (right), who scored the other three goals, giving him 30 goals for the season, celebrate with Cook after the game.

(Right) CLEVELAND 2, HERSHEY 0, 1958

During the final minute of the 2nd-place Barons' 2-0 win over the first-place Hershey Bears on Wednesday, February 19, 1958 before 6,113 at the Arena, the two teams squared off in a free-for-all with gloves and sticks littering the ice around the Hershey goal. Goalie Johnny Bower tied a club record with his eighth shutout.

The Calder Cup-Winning
1953 Cleveland Barons

After clinching the Western Division title, the 1953 Cleveland Barons battled the Pittsburgh Hornets for the Calder Cup in the final round of the American Hockey League playoffs. Tied at three game apiece, the seventh, and deciding game, was played on Thursday, April 16th before 8,688 at the Arena. After three periods of play, the game was deadlocked at 0-0, forcing the game into overtime. The Barons won, 1-0, when 23-year-old Bob Chrystal's winning goal, a magical 70-foot soft lob, bounced oddly off Hornet goalie Gil Mayer for the score. **(Above right)** Capt. Jackie Gordon displays the AHL Calder Cup with coach Bun Cook after the win. **(Right)** Goalie Johnny Bower on the 16th.

(Left) THE CALDER CUP CHAMPIONS

(Bottom): Goalie Johnny Bower, Bob Bailey, Cal Stearns, Ike Hildebrand, Bob Chrystal, Fred Glover, trainer Charlie Homenuke (back row): Ott Heller, Red Williams, Glen Sonmor, Ray Ross, Steve Wochy, captain Jackie Gordon, coach Bun Cook, Eddie Olson, Fred Shero and Ray Ceresino.

(Left) DEFENDING THE CALDER CUP, September 30, 1964

On Thursday, April 25, 1963, the Cleveland Barons beat the Quebec Aces, 5-2, to capture the Calder Cup playoffs in four straight, before an overflow throng of 10,016 at Cleveland Arena. On Wednesday, September 30, 1964, with less than two weeks to go before the season opener, general manager Jackie Gordon's club, training for their American Hockey League title defense in Montreal, Canada, was counting on another year of solid play from veteran starters Bill Needham (left), Cecil Hoekstra, player-coach Fred Glover, Dick Matiussi and Ron Atwell (right).

(Right) THE NATIONAL HOCKEY LEAGUE CLEVELAND BARONS, October 19, 1976

The Cleveland Barons evened their Adams Division-record at 2-2-2 after beating the veteran Chicago Black Hawks on Tuesday, October 19, 1976. Press reporter Bob Schlesinger wrote the following day, "The 5653 fans who went to the hockey game last night didn't get to see Bobby Orr, the Incomparable One. But if the Barons continue to play the way they did at the Coliseum in beating Chicago, 3-0, it may begin to become less important to the crowds which name players are coming to town with the enemy." **(Right)** Jim Pappin, who scored one of the Cleveland goals, fires on Black Hawks goalie Tony Esposito in the second period. Another goal was scored by Dennis Maruk, raising his season-opening output to five goals and five assists in six games. Barons goalie Giles Meloche stopped 31 shots for the shutout.

Basketball in Cleveland

(Left) MILWAUKEE 112, CINCINNATI 92, January 13, 1970

A new attendance high for a National Basketball Association game at Cleveland Arena was set on Tuesday, January 13, 1970, when 11,197 watched 22-year-old rookie sensation Lew Alcindor and the Milwaukee Bucks battle the Cincinnati Royals. Milwaukee raised its record to 31-15 by easily outdistancing the Royals 112-92. **(Left)** Alcindor, who finished with 13 rebounds and 28 points- 18 in the second half- launches one of his patented sky hooks over Connie Dierking (24), and Fred Foster (15). Veteran guard Oscar Robertson scored 17 points for the Royals.

(Below) THE CAVS' FIRST PRACTICE, September 8, 1970

"An NBA Franchise is Born," offered the headline on Wednesday, September 9, 1970, to a story by Press sports reporter Bob August, who wrote, "This was a historic occasion, an official launching into troubled waters, and it seemed that Nick Mileti should

have risen to the challenge with a dramatic flourish, something like breaking a bottle of champagne on the prow of a seven foot center. Instead they merely dribbled some basketballs out on the floor of the Baldwin-Wallace College gym and started throwing them at the baskets and a franchise was born. The Cleveland Cavaliers, founded in 1970, official colors wine and gold, hopes high and future uncertain. There were 19 players out there- with two missing and excused, under the watchful eye of coach Bill Fitch." **(Above)** Fitch addresses his players during the first practice session on Tuesday, September 8th. Fitch remarked, "The closest thing we have to regulars would be Len Chappell and McCoy McLemore, who started some last season and have been regulars sometime in their careers." August added after the quote, "Chappell and McLemore have records that read more like Greyhound bus tables."

(Left) CLEVELAND 119, BOSTON 117, January 25, 1971

It took a 22-foot last-second jumper by Dave Sorenson to give the rookie Cavaliers their eighth win of the season, a thrilling 119-117 upset victory over coach Tommy Heinsohn's Boston Celtics before 3,323 screaming Cleveland Arena fans on Monday, January 25, 1971. The win was the club's second over an established team, raising their season record to 8-47. Though veteran guard John Havlicek scored 29 for the Celtics, Cavs guard Bingo Smith led all players with 31 points. **(Left)** Walt Wesley (left), Luther Rackley and McCoy McLemore (right), who led the team with nine rebounds, leave the court after beating the veteran Celtics.

(Right) UPSETTING THE LAKERS, March 22, 1972

The powerful Los Angeles Lakers (67-13), led by veterans Jerry West, Wilt Chamberlain, Happy Hairston, Gail Goodrich and Jim McMillan, faced the Cavaliers (23-56), before 10,819 at the Arena on Wednesday, March 22, 1972. Led by ex-Laker Rick Roberson, who grabbed 14 rebounds and scored a career-high 29 points, the young Cavs upset their elders, 124-120, for the biggest win in their two-year history. **(Right)** Guard Austin Carr (far left), who scored 9 points, salutes the crowd after the win. With Carr are West, Goodrich (each scored 31 points), and forward John Johnson, who scored 28 points. Cavs Bingo Smith and Butch Beard added 27 and 24 points. The Lakers, riding an eight-game win streak, would have tied the record for most NBA wins with a victory.

CLEVELAND			
Beard	9	6-7	24
Carr	4	1-3	9
Johnson	8	12-12	28
Roberson	12	5-8	29
Smith	12	3-4	27
Sorenson	1	0-0	2
Washington	0	1-1	1
Wesley	2	0-0	4

(Below) CLEVELAND 91, PORTLAND 80, December 2, 1975

The next day's headline read, "Psst...Austin's back and toolin' pretty well," after the Cavaliers, with a season high 19 points and 16 rebounds from forward Jim Chones, beat the Portland Trail Blazers, 91-80, on Tuesday, December 2, 1975 before 7,087, the season's smallest turnout at Richfield Coliseum. Carr, playing his third game after coming off knee surgery, scored 10 points in 21 minutes of action. At left, "The Great Intimidator," newly-acquired center Nate Thurmond, blocks the path of Portland's Sydney Wicks. Nate, "rapidly becoming a fan favorite," according to Press writer Burt Graeff, scored 11 points with nine rebounds. At far right is forward Jim Brewer, who scored 12 points.

1975-76
"A Miracle Season"

(Right)
CLEVELAND 106, BOSTON 87, May 14, 1976

Played before a soldout Coliseum house of 21,564 on Friday, May 14, 1976, the Cavaliers accomplished the unbelievable, upending the veteran Boston Celtics, 106-87, to even the Eastern Conference playoff series at 2-2. **(Right)** Cavaliers head coach Bill Fitch shouts instructions to his bench, including forward Bingo Smith (far right), who scored 27 points. The series moved from Cleveland to Boston where the Celtics prevailed.

CLEVELAND 83, WASHINGTON 78, February 9, 1976

A new attendance mark was set at Richfield Coliseum on Sunday, February 9, 1976, when 21,130 watched the Cavaliers, with five players in double figures, beat the star-studded Washington Bullets, 83-78. **(Below)** Cavs forward Campy Russell (center), breaks to the basket for a pass from teammate Dick Snyder past the Bullets' Phil Chenier (left), and Wes Unseld. The win put Cleveland in a tie for first place with the Bullets. Snyder led the Cavs with 16 points, while Russell finished with 12 points.

(Lower left)
CLEVELAND 120, ATLANTA 92, April 4, 1976

"I wanted Luke to get some playing time tonight and I wanted to light a fire, too. People love him," remarked head coach Bill Fitch (with arms crossed), after 7-2 back-up center Luke Witte, going into the game at left, helped lift the Cavaliers to a 120-92 win over the Atlanta Hawks before 8,430 at the Coliseum on Sunday, April 4, 1976. "Luuuuke, The People's Choice," scored two points in nine minutes of play. Austin Carr led the first-place Cavs with 27 points.

The Death of James (Jimmy) Doyle June 24, 1947

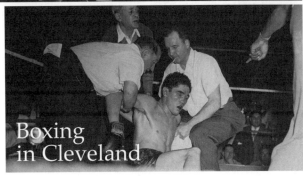

Cleveland's first world championship bout since since 1931 attracted a near-capacity crowd of 11,275 to Cleveland Arena on Tuesday, June 24, 1947, when welterweight champion Sugar Ray Robinson, in his first title defense since outpointing Tommy Bell of Youngstown seven months earlier, fought James (Jimmy) Doyle of Los Angeles. In the 8th round of the scheduled 15-rounder, Robinson (standing above right), began pumping his left steadily into Jimmy's reddened face. A right to the side of the head partly turned Doyle around and left his jaw open for a finishing left hook that "dropped on Jimmy's chin like a bolt from the blue." As Doyle fell, his head bounced twice on the mat, which doctors said probably caused the most damage. **(Right)** Doyle's handlers pull the battered fighter back to his corner. **(Above)** Doyle is carried by stretcher to a waiting ambulance. He was taken to St. Vincent's Charity Hospital where he died after undergoing brain surgery. On Monday, June 30th, coroner Samuel R. Gerber ruled Doyle's death as accidental stating, "Testimony of Doyle's brother Edward Delaney and from information from several sports writers throughout the country indicate that there was a recognizable change in Doyle's personality after the (Arte) Levine fight. However, it was impossible for the examining physicians to find a permanent physical injury."

Boxing in Cleveland

(Left) WITH JIM BROWN, January 29, 1967 Sunday, January 29, 1967 was "Jim Brown Farewell Day," at Cleveland Arena as the former Browns fullback was honored by his peers including Bobby Mitchell, Ernie Green, Leroy Kelly, Gary Collins, Bill Russell, Gene Hickerson, Gayle Sayers, heavyweight champ Cassius (Muhammad Ali) Clay and Sam Huff, who told the crowd of 4,580, "My trip here is to make sure Jim Brown won't be back." At left Brown, with wife Sue, shakes hands with Clay, who told the crowd, "He's still pretty, I am glad to see him retire undefeated," after calling Brown, "the greatest athlete in history next to me." Clay, who was training for a fight with Ernie Terrell the following week, appeared at a Giant Tiger store earlier in the day. Brown's #32 jersey was formally retired at the event.

Muhammad Ali

(Right) THE ALI-WEPNER FIGHT, March 24, 1975

The first heavyweight title fight held in Cleveland took place on Friday, July 3, 1931, when Max Schmeling beat Young Stribling to open the city's new Municipal Stadium. Schmeling took out Stribling with just 19 seconds left in the 15th round. History almost repeated itself on Monday, March 24, 1975, when more than 15,000 at Richfield Coliseum, including 60-year-old former heavyweight champ Joe Louis, watched Muhammad Ali take out Chuck Wepner with only 15 seconds left in the 15th round.

SUGAR RAY ROBINSON & JOE LOUIS
July 3, 1948

Boxers Sugar Ray Robinson (left), dressed in "screaming yellow knickers, a yellow knitted sweater, yellow stockings and dark tan felt hat," and Joe Louis (right), were among the star attractions at the Sixth City Golf Association's National Invitational Tournament at Seneca Country Club on Saturday, July 3, 1948.

Former Browns players, Dante Lavelli and Otto Graham (left), former Browns fullback Marion Motley (lower left), and Lou "The Toe" Groza (below), enjoyed a day on the links at Pine Ridge Country Club during the Cleveland Touchdown Club's annual golf outing on Thursday, July 17, 1958.

(Below) Cleveland Browns head coach Paul Brown (left), checks his scorecard with Western Reserve coach Eddie Finnigan during the Touchdown Club's annual golf outing at Pine Ridge Country Club on Thursday, July 11, 1957.

On the Links in Cleveland

(Below) LITTLE WINS THE NATIONAL OPEN AT CANTERBURY, June 9, 1940

Lawson Little (left), who received $1,000 for his victory, shakes hands of Gene Sarazen after beating Sarazen in an 18-hole playoff on Sunday, June 9, 1940, to win the 44th National Open golf championship before some 5,000 at Canterbury Golf Club. With the two golfers is Harold W. Pierce, president of the United States Golf Association. Finishing behind Little and Sarazen were Horton Smith, Craig Wood, Lloyd Mangrum, Ralph Guldahl, Byron Nelson and Ben Hogan. Ed (Porky) Oliver had tied the two leaders for the lead, but was disqualified.

(Above) ARNIE WINS THE CLEVELAND OPEN AT BEECHMONT, July 1, 1963

Going into the final round of the Cleveland Open at Beechmont Country Club on Sunday, June 30, 1963, Arnold Palmer, Jack Nicklaus & Tony Lema were tied for the lead at 205, with Gary Player one stroke behind. After 72 holes of regulation play, Palmer (left), Lema (second from right), and Tommy Aaron (right), finished in a three-way tie at 273, forcing an 18-hole playoff. On Monday, July 1st, 5,000 watched Palmer beat Aaron and Lema to win his fifth tournament of the year by a three-stroke margin. The $22,000 winner's check boosted Palmer's gross tournament earnings for the year to $85,545, a new high in P. G. A. winnings. With the three men is fellow golfer Jack Burke.

(Left) 1946 CATHEDRAL LATIN LIONS

As fall practice began for the Cathedral Latin Lions on Monday, August 26, 1946, returning to the Lions offense were (front row): Tom Bohn, George Raggets, John Beletic, Al Hassello, Dan Smerritt, (top row): George Werling, Cliff Hill, Emory Csizma, Bob Matoney and John Petricig. After winning the East Senate, the Lions captured their fourth straight city title on November 23rd, beating Holy Name, 35-6, in the annual Charity Game before a record crowd of 70,955 at Municipal Stadium. HB Emory Csizma rushed for 167 yards in the win.

Playing High School Football

(Left) AUGIE BOSSU'S 1955 BENEDICTINE BENGALS

The Benedictine Bengals (left), not only won the Senate crown, but also captured the city championship under first-year head coach Augie Bossu. Playing in the first Thanksgiving Day Charity Game at Municipal Stadium, Benedictine beat the St. Ignatius Wildcats, 47-6, before 21,029 on Thursday, November 24, 1955, for the first of three straight city titles. Game MVP Tom Rini (77), scored three touchdowns.

(Right) HOLY NAME WINS THE SENATE TITLE, November 14, 1961 "Hail the Champs! Holy Name No. 1," read The Press sports page headline on Wednesday, November 15, 1961, after the undefeated Holy Name Green Wave beat the St. Ignatius Wildcats, 14-6, to capture the Senate title playoff before 7,300 at West Tech. At right, coach Carl Falivene's victorious Green Wave celebrate after beating the Wildcats on a 26-yard TD pass from HB Frank Solich to end Mike Fiorentino and a 61-yard Solich TD run. Star FB Mike Worley (23), gained 73 yards for the Green Wave. On November 23rd, Holy Name beat Cathedral Latin, 12-0, on two Solich TDs, to capture the city title.

(Left) ST. IGNATIUS WINS THE CITY TITLE, November 26, 1964

On Thursday, November 26, 1964, the St. Ignatius Wildcats battled coach Augie Bossu's Benedictine Bengals in the 34th annual Charity Game at Municipal Stadium. St. Ignatius captured the school's 29th victory in the last 30 games, manhandling the Bengals, 48-6. All-Scholastic QB Brian Dowling (#15 lower right), led the Wildcats by tossing four TD passes and scoring twice on 71-yard and two-yard runs. The St. Ignatius squad later presented an autographed game ball to the widow of popular Wildcat line coach Ab Strosnider, who passed away less than a month before the title match. The St. Ignatius players wore black armbands in memory of their coach.

Jesse Owens at East Tech, 1933

Though he was performing with a wrap around his left knee, East Tech's Jesse Owens set a new state and national scholastic broad jump record with a leap of 24 feet, 3 inches during a triangular meet with East High and Cathedral Latin at John Adams Field on Friday, April 28, 1933. Owens' record jump bettered any jump he had ever made and surpassed his own state record by 15 inches. (The world record at the time was just under 26 feet). In addition to his record-breaking performance in the broad jump, Owens also won the 220-yard dash with a time of 22.7 seconds and the 100-yard dash with a time of 9.9 seconds. Helped by Owens' three wins and the stellar performance of teammate Dave Albritton, who captured the low and high hurdles,

the high jump and finished second in the broad jump, coach Ed Weil's East Tech squad easily outpaced its two competitors for the win. **(Above)** Owens makes his record-setting leap during the triangular meet at John Adams.

(Left) East Tech's world record-holding 880-yard relay team of Dave Albritton (standing), Jerry Williams (sitting), Alfred Storey and Jesse Owens met with track coach Ed Weil at John Adams Field before heading to Chicago for the national scholastic track and field meet on Saturday, June 17, 1933. East Tech won the national scholastic title, as Owens not only equalled the world record of 9.4 seconds in winning the 100-yard dash, but also shattered scholastic records in winning the 220-yard dash and the broad jump with a leap of 24 feet, 9 inches. In addition, Albritton won the high jump title by leaping 6 feet, 2 inches and finished third in the high hurdles. East Tech added additional points with a second-place finish in the 880-yard relay.

(Right)
MARKING ATHLETIC EXCELLENCE AT EAST TECH HIGH, May 4, 1951

Four decades of scholastic triumphs by East Tech High athletes were represented by the impressive trophy display at right, organized for an upcoming open house at the school on Friday, May 4, 1951. Kneeling with one of the over 400 trophies is former Scarabs legend Harrison Dillard, who starred at East Tech, Baldwin-Wallace College and in the Olympics. Dillard won a gold medal at the 1948 London Olympic Games in the 100-meter dash, and captured gold again at the 1952 Olympic Games in Helsinki, Finland by winning the 110-meter high hurdles. The trophy display featured awards from all scholastic athletic endeavors including track, basketball, swimming, football and baseball.

Now in our third printing!

From Our "Everything Cleveland" Book Shelf

MUST HAVE FOR SPORTS FANS!

MUNICIPAL STADIUM
Memories on the Lakefront® VOLUME 1
A 50-YEAR PICTORIAL HISTORY 1931 TO 1981

Featuring over 420 images from the Cleveland Press Collection
EDITED BY GEORGE CORMACK

BOOK SECTIONS

• The Beginning Years 1930-1931
• The First Professional Baseball Game, 1932
• Municipal Stadium 1933-1939
• Baseball at the Stadium 1940-45
• Football at the Stadium 1945-49
• The Bill Veeck Era 1946-49
• Municipal Stadium The 1950's
• Notre Dame vs. Navy 1932-52
• Municipal Stadium The 1960's
• Municipal Stadium 1970-1981
• City High School Football
  (The Charity Games) 1931-1970

Over 420 photographs 1931-81

150 pages, covering each decade from the 30's to the 1981.

Soft Cover 81/2" x 11"

**Baseball Fans-
Over 90 starting lineups
listed from 1932-1981!**

Suggested Retail: $18.95

**OVER 350 PEOPLE, PLACES AND EVENTS ARE
FEATURED IN THIS UNIQUE HISTORY BOOK-**

• Jack Lemmon • Billy Wilder • Brian Sipe • Stella Walsh • High School Charity Games • Tris Speaker • Al Rosen • Nap Lajoie • Earl Averill • Paul Brown • Cy Young • Brian Dowling • Bob Feller • Max Schmeling • Herb Score • Notre Dame • Satchel Paige • Ray Fosse • Ted Williams • Lou Boudreau • Milt Plum • Dennis Eckersley • Joe DiMaggio • Ty Cobb • 1935 National Eucharistic Congress • Sonny Siebert • Rocky Colavito • Franklin Lewis • Oscar Vitt • Rev. Msr. Fulton J. Sheen • Larry Doby • Otto Graham • Jim Brown • 1972 Billy Graham Crusade • Greg Pruitt • Gaylord Perry • Mel Harder • Mike Garcia • 1942 Army War Show • Babe Ruth • Bishop Joseph Schrembs • Dante Lavelli • Bob Waterfield • Leroy Kelly • Lou "The Toe" Groza • Gary Collins • 1936 Stadium Gas Explosion • Marion Motley • Johnny Allen • Frank Ryan • Bill Nelsen • Frank Lane • Mike Phipps • Bill Veeck, Jr. • Walter Johnson • Nick Mileti • Buddy Bell • Bobby Avila • Clay Matthews • Jim Ninowski • William Duggan • Pat Seerey • Pelé • Bob Hope • Gary Hansley • Gale Sayers • John L. Severance • Charlie Jamieson • Charley Lupica • Bill Wambsganss • Jimmie Foxx • Ray Mack • Tony Galento • Benny Goodman • Connie Mack • Ann Blyth • Festivals of Freedom • 1947 Midget Race• Ladies' Day • Dale Mitchell • Joe and June Earley • Mickey McBride • Luke Easter • Allie Reynolds • Mickey Mantle • Billy Martin • Roger Maris • Casey Stengel • Al Lopez • Jimmy Piersall • Early Wynn • John Romano • Bob Lemon • Mike Hargrove • Frank Robinson • Joe Charboneau • Len Barker • Dom Grassie • Bob Konkoly • Mike Hegan • Greg Marn • Glen Novak • John Wirtz • Dean Chance • Mrs. Knute Rockne • Larry Zelina • Don Miller • Elmer Layden • Tom Matte • Willie Mays • 1936 Balloon Race • Chuck Noll • Mac Speedie • John Adams • Woody Hayes • Rocco Scotti • Hugo Zacchini • Blanton Collier • Joe Namath •

instant CONCEPTS INC.

Publishers of annual
HISTORY OF CLEVELAND
AND CLEVELAND SPORTS
HISTORY CALENDARS

WATCH FOR OUR
UPCOMING WEBSITE!

CALL, WRITE, E.MAIL OR FAX US TODAY!

(440) 891-1964 • FAX (440) 826-1920 • 1-800-644-7769 • e.mail. calendar@infinet.com

PHOTOGRAPH CREDITS

The Cleveland Press newspaper operated as an afternoon daily in various formats from Nov. 2, 1878 to June 17, 1982. The photographs found in this book salute the work done by these former Cleveland Press photographers.

Frank Aleksandrowicz   Larry Nighswander
Fred Bottomer   Bernie Noble
Tom Brunton   Frank Reed
Timothy Culek   Larry Rubenstein
Van Dillard   Ted R. Schneider, Jr.
Byron Filkins   Herman Seid
John Goski   Paul Tepley
Peter Hastings   James Thomas
Jerry Horton   Bob Tomsic
Walter Kneal   Tony Tomsic
Clayton Knipper   Paul Toppelstein
Ron Kuntz   Louis Van Oeyen
James Mell   Glenn Zahn
Lou Moore
John Nash
Bill Nehez

Information on specific photographs can be obtained by contacting Instant Concepts at (440) 891-1964 or by fax at (440) 826-1920.

GETTING THE PICTURE, Circa 1930
Cleveland Press photographer Byron Filkins (second from right), with Bob Sable, Eddie Johnson and Gordon Richardson inside League Park.